WOMEN AND
POLITICAL PARTICIPATION

WOMEN AND POLITICAL PARTICIPATION

Cultural Change in the Political Arena

M. Margaret Conway
UNIVERSITY OF FLORIDA

Gertrude A. Steuernagel
KENT STATE UNIVERSITY

David W. Ahern
UNIVERSITY OF DAYTON

A Division of Congressional Quarterly Inc.
Washington, D.C.

For Robin and Jean Gibson
M.M.C.

For Scott and Sky—the heart of me
G.S.

For my mother, Janet Ahern
D.A.

Library of Congress Cataloging-in-Publication Data

Conway, M. Margaret (Mary Margaret), 1935–
    Women and political participation : cultural change in the political arena /
M. Margaret Conway, Gertrude A. Steuernagel, David W. Ahern.
    p. cm.
    Includes bibliographical references and index.
    ISBN 0-87187-922-0
    1. Women in politics--United States. I. Steuernagel, Gertrude A.
II. Ahern, David W.   III. Title.
HQ1236.5.U6C65 1997
306.2'082--dc21   97-21580

Contents

Tables, Figures, and Boxes

FIGURES

BOXES

Preface

This book about women's political participation in the United States focuses on the effects of cultural change on gender roles and the impact of role perception on women's political attitudes and political behavior.

In many ways, the story of women's political participation is the story of cultural change. This point is well illustrated by one woman's description of her awakening political interests. Barbara Boxer was not politically active until spurred by the assassination of Robert Kennedy but won election to the U.S. Senate two decades later. She remarked: "[My husband] must have felt like he married Debbie Reynolds and woke up with Eleanor Roosevelt!"[1]

At any point in our history culture influences our perception of women in part through the presentation of images. Any culture presents a variety of images of women, and these images affect people's thinking. A culture can present no images of women as leaders, thus sending a message that women cannot lead; or it can present images of women as religious leaders but not as political leaders, suggesting that some areas of leadership are open to women but not others.

However, cultural images evolve, often reflecting the confusion that results when society experiences change—such as in popular notions of what women appropriately can and cannot do. For example, the "waif look," which was popular among fashion models in the early 1990s, suggested that women are childlike and frail—the opposite of the image evoked by the women who attained positions of power in the congressional elections of 1992. The "waifs" may have been a cultural response to women's increasing involvement in political affairs. The image may even have served as a safety valve for some of the dissent and anxiety surrounding such a major cultural change. What is clear is that this image of women coexisted with, rather than replaced, the newly emerging image of women as political activists.

In this book we explore women's political participation in the context of cultural change; we believe that this context is critical to understanding women and political participation. Chapter 1 is an introduction to women's status in a liberal culture and a survey of women's political participation from colonial times to 1920. Women's notions of gender role, appropriate behavior and attitudes, and gender identity are the subjects of Chapter 2, which includes a discussion of childhood and adult political learning, with particular emphasis on acculturation and political socialization. In Chapter 3 we examine the gender gap in political attitudes and historical trends in women's political attitudes. Chapter 4 is an analysis of the relationship between trends in women's political attitudes and in their social attitudes, the influence of changing cultural images of women, and changes in people's political attitudes. In Chapter 5 we consider the gender gap in voting, historical trends in women's voting behavior, and the effects of changes in women's roles on their turnout to vote and their vote choice. Chapter 6 focuses on the cultural construction of images of women as political leaders (as members of political parties, in political campaigns, and as officeholders) and the implications of these images for women's political leadership. The impact of women's participation on politics and public policy is assessed in Chapter 7.

This book will be of interest to students of American politics and women's studies. We hope it helps to strengthen a movement, begun in the 1970s, to make gender a serious subject of study in political science, for academic discourse contributes to the cultural construction of images of women. Gender has always been a politically relevant subject, even though political scientists have sometimes ignored it; and American women have always been politically involved, even when political scientists ignored them. Although political science as a discipline no longer overlooks women, relatively little has been published about them. From 1906 to 1991, the *American Political Science Review,* for example, published only twenty-four articles pertaining to women.[2]

An effort has been made to make the material in this book accessible to students, with suggestions for further reading for those wishing to pursue particular topics. Since often the academic literature lags behind the media and the culture in identifying cultural change, we have included stories from real life to demonstrate that cultural change can affect individual lives often before it is recognized as a trend by analysts.

Some of the data used in this book were made available by the InterUniversity Consortium for Political and Social Research. The data for the American National Election Studies were collected by the Center for Political Studies, Institute for Social Research, University of Michigan, under grants funded by the National Science Foundation. Neither the original collectors of the data nor the Consortium bear any responsibility for the analyses or interpretations presented here.

M. Margaret Conway gratefully acknowledges the research support provided by the Robin and Jean Gibson Term Professorship, College of Liberal Arts, University of Florida, during the 1995–1996 academic year.

The authors acknowledge the contributions of Brenda Carter and Talia Greenberg of CQ Press to the completion of this project and of Lydia Jeanne Duncan, an outstanding manuscript editor.

We would also like to thank Barbara Norrander, Nancy H. Zingale, and an anonymous reviewer, whose comments helped us revise the manuscript.

NOTES

1. Barbara Boxer with Nicole Boxer, *Strangers in the Senate: Politics and the New Revolution of Women in America* (Washington, D.C.: National Press Books, 1994), 69.

2. Rita Mae Kelly and Kimberly Fisher, "An Assessment of Articles About Women in the 'Top 15' Political Science Journals," *PS: Political Science and Politics* 26, no. 3 (September 1993): 544.

CHAPTER 1

Women, Culture, and Political Participation

ELEANORA'S STORY

Eleanora Tomec, born in Pittsburgh in 1910, was the only one of seven siblings to survive past the age of 5.[1] She began to work as a secretary immediately after graduating from the eighth grade. Eleanora's Slovenian immigrant parents encouraged her in her efforts to continue her education. She obtained a high school diploma by attending night school and then enrolled in a few college classes. So eager were her parents for her to be part of their adopted homeland, however, that they refused to teach her to speak Slovenian, insisting that she speak English "like a good American girl."

Eleanora became engaged to a local man and they married in 1945, after he returned from military service in World War II. Thus she was 35 at the time of her marriage, not 20 or 21, the typical ages of women who married for the first time in 1945.[2] The year of her marriage was also the year when the divorce rate reached its highest level of the century.[3] Eleanora continued to work as a secretary until their first child, a girl, was born in 1946. Eleanora was fairly typical in this respect. The birth rate in 1946, 23.3 births per 1,000 population, was the highest since 1921.[4] Her second daughter was born in 1948. Both Eleanora and her husband felt they had to "keep trying" until they had the son they so much wanted. Despite her age, Eleanora had a third child, a boy, in 1951. She remained out of the paid work force until he entered kindergarten, then returned to work as a secretary on a part-time basis. By 1960, she was working full time. In that year, 49.9 percent of the women in her age group, 45 to 54, were in the labor force on a full- or part-time basis, compared with 95.7 percent of the men in that age group.[5] Although Eleanora was somewhat typical in this regard in 1960, she had not been so earlier in her working life. In 1940, when Eleanora was 30, 95.2 percent of the men aged 25 to 34 but only 32.9 percent of the women aged 25 to 34 were members of the labor force.[6]

Eleanora's earnings were earmarked for her children's education. All three graduated from college, but she and her husband had made certain that their son went to a prestigious school, whereas the daughters, both of whom had academic records superior to that of their brother, attended a nearby state university. The daughter who challenged the justice of this decision was told by her father that she was fortunate to attend any college since the family "had a boy to educate."

Eleanora died of breast cancer in 1974, two years after her radical mastectomy and radiation therapy. Treatment options were not discussed with her or her family, and the biopsy and surgery were performed in a single operation. She lived to see her children graduate from college, but died before the births of her three grandchildren. In 1974, 26.8 of every 100,000 American women died of breast cancer.[7]

Many cultural changes occurred during Eleanora's lifetime. She was born ten years before passage of the Nineteenth Amendment guaranteed the right to vote for all American women; the education she received was limited but exceeded that of her parents. Although she spent her working life in a traditional female occupation, she was one of the few women in her neighborhood who worked full time while their children were young. During World War II, Eleanora continued to work as a secretary, seemingly uninterested in better-paying defense jobs such as that held by "Rosie the Riveter." The era that encompassed most of her working years was one in which women's status had not yet become a public policy issue. The Equal Pay Act of 1963 and Title VII of the Civil Rights Act of 1964 (which outlawed sexual discrimination in employment) thus had little impact on her life. A devout Catholic, she opposed abortion but was too ill at the time to take much interest in the *Roe v. Wade* decision (1973). When she detected the lump in her breast and went to have it examined, she did not question the doctor's decision that a radical mastectomy should be done immediately if the biopsy were positive. When she awoke from the anesthetic, she was told that the lump had been malignant and that the surgery had already been performed.

Politically, Eleanora, like her parents and husband, was a Democrat. Unlike many women at that time, she voted regularly. Adlai Stevenson, the Democratic presidential candidate in 1952 and 1956, was her political hero, although she was troubled by his divorce. She supported John Kennedy, the Democratic presidential candidate in 1960, in large part because he was a Catholic. Eleanora was not a joiner and belonged to no community groups. She was never involved in any form of legal or illegal protest activity, but she did support her children in their antiwar activities. One of her daughters claimed that she knew the United States' involvement in Vietnam had lost popular support when she overheard her mother bragging to her father that, of all the children of the Saturday morning regulars at Teresa Eppolito's House of Beauty, one of theirs had been the first in town to march in Washington, D.C.

Politically, Eleanora identified with party and faith, not gender. She wanted her daughters to be able to make choices about education and career but often felt distanced from them. It was Eleanora's commitment, emotionally and financially, to her daughters' education that made possible their college degrees. She both gloried in and despaired over their independence. In her mind, her older daughter's wedding assumed mythic proportions because it was the only sign that either of the two young women was interested in maintaining a traditional lifestyle. If Eleanora was at all aware of the women's movement, she never made mention of it to her family.

The story of Eleanora and her family is one of personal and cultural change. As such, it is the story of American women's political participation, for the story of American women's political participation is one of cultural change. Culture can be defined as "a core of traditional ideas, practices, and technology shared by a people."[8] This focus on culture is based on the idea that what matters to individuals—what affects their political attitudes, for example—is learned through their interaction with the people and institutions they encounter throughout their lives.[9]

Eleanora played many roles during her lifetime: dutiful daughter, efficient employee, loyal wife and companion, and responsible mother. Both she and the roles underwent change in that period. All in all, politics had little meaning for her. This is not to say, however, that she had no political opinions. Each of her three children was educated in a parochial school, and she was intent on ensuring that state and local governments not be involved in administrating these schools. She acknowledged she and her husband would have to pay their property taxes to support the public schools while also paying tuition for private schools. Although she lived most of her life in segregated white neighborhoods, she was in favor of integration. She came to oppose the war in Vietnam and told her family that should her son be drafted, she would want him to flee to Canada. Eleanora thought that homosexuality was a perversion, marriage was forever, and the United States was the best place in the world to live and raise a family. She died before environmentalism became a household word. She had no objection to paying taxes to support poor families, but she believed that too many people were too lazy to work.

What did political participation mean to Eleanora? She viewed herself as a good citizen because she tried to stay informed and voted in primaries and general elections. Occasionally she would donate money to a Democratic candidate. But she never wrote a letter to a governmental official or put a political bumper sticker on her car.

WOMEN'S STATUS IN A LIBERAL CULTURE

There are a number of ways to describe the culture that influenced Eleanora and her fellow citizens. It is most commonly defined as "liberal." A liberal culture values individuality, freedom, and equality. Politically, it embraces democracy; economically, it is based on capitalism. What people in a liberal culture do with their lives is their concern, so long as their actions do not harm others or infringe on their rights.[10] Government is supposed to act as a referee and is not supposed to give special treatment to any person or group. A liberal culture, however, does not require continuous, intense political participation, defined as "those activities of citizens that attempt to influence the structure of government, the selection of government authorities, or the policies of government."[11] What is required is that the right to participate politically not be abridged. From this perspective, a liberal culture does not necessarily consider lack of political participation as negative.

Women's status in this liberal culture has changed over time, as has the culture itself.[12] The contrasts between Eleanora's life and the lives of her daughters are indicative of these changes. Although Eleanora worked throughout much of her adulthood, her job took second place to that of her husband; she thought of her work as a job and of her husband's work as a career. When he had to relocate because of work-related interests, Eleanora moved with him; it was taken for granted that she would take time away from work for child rearing. During the time she stayed home with the children she was not a member of the paid work force. As a result, she never accumulated enough time in any one job to earn a pension. Eleanora's older daughter left a promising career upon the birth of her first child. Throughout her marriage she assumed the traditional roles of homemaker and mother. Unlike Eleanora, however, she did consider alternatives. She remained out of the work force for almost twenty years, reentering only at the time of her divorce. Although she had a college degree, her skills had become obsolete and her first job on returning to the work force was a low-paying clerical one. The younger daughter, in contrast, worked continually after completing graduate school. She married late and had a child late in her childbearing years, but neither event caused her to leave the work force for more than two weeks. Her husband adjusted his career to hers, and both viewed child rearing as a shared responsibility.

Eleanora and her daughters had different ideas about work, marriage, and motherhood. The daughters had educational opportunities that were unavailable to Eleanora. The younger daughter raised her child at a time when there were far more child care options than her mother or sister could ever have imagined. Divorce for Eleanora was never an option, but it was for her older daughter. Eleanora can be said to have been more accepting of a patriarchal society than were her daughters. Although a liberal culture stresses autonomy and self-determination, they have been relative concepts, not always applicable in theory or practice to everyone. Before the Civil War, for example, many white Americans justified the "peculiar institution" of slavery as the best policy for both whites and blacks. Even in the Constitution of the United States, slaves were originally counted as three-fifths of a person for purposes of taxation and representation. And after women were legally recognized as persons, they were not always able to take full advantage of the opportunities of the liberal culture. Women's responsibilities with regard to home and children, for example, could interfere with their ability to act as autonomous beings in the workplace. Eleanora was never denied the right to vote because of her sex, but her life was shaped in a certain way because she was a woman.

WOMEN AND CULTURAL CHANGE

Both Eleanora and her daughters were at some time part of the nation's work force, and this is the trend for all American women. In 1994, 59 percent of American women belonged to the work force; married women were almost as likely as single women to be employed.[13] Approximately four decades earlier, in 1950, only 34 percent of American women were in the work force, and married women were less likely than single women to be employed.[14] Eleanora's younger daughter, who continued to work after her child was born, is part of another trend. In 1994, more than half of all women with children under the age of 6 were in the work force on a full- or part-time basis.[15] Women's areas of employment have not changed as much as have the percentages of women who are now employed. Eleanora spent all of her working years as a secretary. In 1994, 99 percent of all secretaries were female. In 1940, 988,081 women and 68,805 men were employed as stenographers, typists, or secretaries.[16] Eleanora's daughters' occupations reflect the movement of women out of the "pink-collar ghettos," where most women are still employed. Her older daughter was a computer programmer, a profession that in 1994 was 31 percent female. Her younger daughter became a university professor, a profession that in 1994 was 43 percent female.[17]

Eleanora obtained her high school diploma in night school and earned a few college credits. In respect to education, Eleanora was fairly typical of her peers. In 1940, the median number of school years completed by someone in Eleanora's age group (30 to 34) was 9.5. For males, the figure was 9.2 and for females 9.9. In that same age group in 1940, women were more likely than men to have completed high school, but men were more likely than women to have four or more years of college. Interestingly, in that year women were more likely than men to have one to three years of college (as did Eleanora).[18] Her older daughter earned a bachelor's degree and her younger daughter earned bachelor's, master's, and doctoral degrees. Again, the trend in Eleanora's family reflects the broader cultural trend. In the 1990s, more women than men are enrolled in college, more women than men earn bachelor degrees, and more women than men earn master's degrees. Men continue to earn more doctoral degrees than women. More and more women are earning degrees in traditionally male fields such as engineering and business.[19]

Women's political participation has both been affected by and caused cultural change. Women's efforts to change a culture that denied them the right to participate fully in political activities are the subject of the following section.

Women participated in political activities long before the ratification of the Nineteenth Amendment to the Constitution (1920), which established women's right to vote in all federal, state, and local government elections. During the American Revolution, many women joined the Daughters of Liberty and supported the Revolutionary War effort by providing supplies such as food and clothing to soldiers and by persuading women to boycott goods imported from England. Prior to the Civil War, many women in the North were active in the abolitionist movement. Their experiences enabled them to gain the organizational and oratorical skills that many would use in the women's suffrage movement. During the nineteenth century, many women participated in other efforts to affect policy, which included campaigns to establish free public education, to improve the working conditions of women employed in factories (in textiles and other industries), and to gain the right for labor unions to organize. Women also formed organizations with such varied goals as providing charity to the impoverished, lobbying the federal government to create widow's and orphan's pensions for survivors of soldiers killed in the Civil War, and obtaining passage of federal and state laws prohibiting children from working in the nation's factories and mines.[20]

Women's Political Status Prior to Passage of the Nineteenth Amendment

Under common law, which the colonies' founders brought with them from England, women lost all legal rights when they married.[21] Husband and wife became one legal entity upon marriage, and according to English common law the spouse who exercised legal rights for the couple was the husband. He possessed all legal rights including, if he was eligible under colonial law (and later, state law), the right to vote. Single women had few legal rights and did not have the right to vote.[22]

In colonial America, women thus did not have a legally established right to vote. One early request for the voting franchise was presented by

Margaret Brent to the Maryland Council in 1647. A wealthy plantation owner, Margaret Brent was also the agent and representative of Lord Baltimore, the proprietor of the Maryland colony, as well as the executrix of the estate of Leonard Calvert, the deceased brother of Lord Baltimore. She demanded not one vote, but two—the first because she met the colony's property-owning qualifications for voting, and the second because she was the representative of the estate of Leonard Calvert. She argued that if her request was denied, all proceedings of the Maryland House of Burgesses would be invalid. The Maryland Council was not persuaded; it rejected her request.[23]

Abigail Adams of Massachusetts, the wife of John Adams (who later became the second president of the United States), wrote to him in 1787, when he was serving as a member of the convention that was drafting the United States Constitution. She requested that "he remember the ladies" and not put unlimited power in the hands of men.[24] Her request for political rights for women was not considered by the Constitutional Convention.

Despite the lack of formal enfranchisement of women, in several communities women members of some prominent families did vote until state laws were enacted to prohibit their voting. For example, women voted in New Jersey until 1807, when political leaders who feared that women's votes would contribute to their opponents' success enacted a state law prohibiting women from voting in elections.[25]

During the nineteenth century, women in a few states obtained the right to vote in school board elections. In recognition of women's role in child rearing, in 1838 Kentucky became the first state to grant women a limited right to vote; it allowed widows in rural districts who had children in school to vote in school board elections.[26] In 1861 Kansas became the second state to grant women the right to vote in school board elections. By 1900, women were eligible to vote in school board elections in twenty-four states.[27]

Nonetheless, women's political and legal rights were restricted in most states during the nineteenth century. The extension of political rights began in the frontier states and proceeded very slowly. The first full grant of suffrage to women occurred in 1869, when the drafters of the Wyoming territorial constitution enfranchised women in the hope of attracting more of them to settle in that sparsely populated state. When Wyoming became a state in 1890, its constitution stipulated that women had a right to vote in all elections. By 1918 fifteen states (of which thirteen were western states) had granted women the right to vote in all elections; by 1920 an additional thirteen states had granted them the right to vote only in presidential elections.[28]

Why is the right to vote so important? If used effectively, it provides a mechanism by which citizens may influence both who rules and what public policies are implemented. When a group of people who have a common concern votes on the basis of that concern and makes its desires known to political candidates, its actions may have a significant effect on both the campaign promises and the performance in office of those who are elected. The right to vote can thus be a powerful weapon for a group in obtaining its preferred policy outcomes.[29]

The Struggle for Women's Rights and Passage of the Nineteenth Amendment

The struggle that culminated in congressional passage of the Nineteenth Amendment and its ratification by the states lasted more than a century. The organized campaign for women's suffrage can be traced to the involvement of women in the antislavery movement. Two of the founders of that first women's movement, Elizabeth Cady Stanton and Lucretia Mott, attended an international antislavery convention in London in 1840. The United States was represented by both men and women. The convention ruled, however, that the women could not be official delegates and would have to sit in the gallery with the spectators. That incident led Stanton and Mott to spend much of their time in London discussing the legal status and social condition of women; they resolved to work to change them. Both women were married, and Stanton and her large family moved to the small town of Seneca Falls in upstate New York. Because she had almost total responsibility for the daily household and child-rearing tasks (her husband was frequently away on business and she seldom had dependable household help), Stanton had little time to organize a social or political movement.[30]

In 1848 Lucretia Mott and her husband visited friends residing near the Stanton home in Seneca Falls. Stanton and Mott, together with three women friends, decided to call a "convention" to discuss the social, political, and economic conditions of women. They placed a small advertisement in the *Seneca County Courier*, inviting others to attend a women's rights meeting at the Methodist Chapel on July 19 and 20, 1848. Only women were asked to attend the first day of the meeting; men were invited to attend the second day. However, men were present on both days, and James

Mott was asked to chair the meeting, as none of the women who organized the meeting had such experience.[31] The women organizers drafted a Declaration of Principles, which was largely a paraphrase of the Declaration of Independence. Stanton also drafted a set of resolutions designed to implement the Declaration of Principles. The only resolution that was not passed unanimously was Resolution 9: "Resolved that it is the duty of the women of this country to secure their sacred right to the elective franchise." The idea of the vote for women was so controversial that the resolution passed by only a small margin.[32] Of the sixty-eight women who signed the Declaration of Principles in 1848, only one lived to cast a ballot in 1920.[33]

The Seneca Falls Convention can be considered the beginning of the organized women's suffrage movement in the United States. It was not, however, the first women's movement. Since the founding of the republic under the Constitution of 1787, many women had joined the struggle to obtain other rights, such as the right to an education, the right to manage their own property after marriage, and the right to have custody of and guardianship over their children in the event of a divorce.

Married women had few rights in any of the states. If they worked outside the home, they did not have the right to control their own earnings. The husband had the right of guardianship over children. Property earned or acquired during the marriage by the wife was controlled by the husband. It could be disposed of in any way he wished—sold, given, or gambled away.[34]

Few women were given the opportunity to obtain an education. Because they were believed to be frail, frivolous, and less mentally capable than men, an education in academic subjects was considered neither socially appropriate nor within women's intellectual capabilities. Free public education did not exist at the beginning of the nineteenth century, and until well into that century, most of the private schools that existed for women were designed to teach them the social graces and household management skills. The negative view of education for women was not held by all; some (both women and men) believed that women were as intellectually capable as men. In 1819, Emma Willard petitioned the New York State Assembly for a charter for a women's school and for a financial subsidy to establish a "female seminary" for young women. She received the charter but not the subsidy, and in 1821 she opened the Troy Female Seminary in Troy, New York. However, even when schools for girls were established, the general lack of public funding for girls' education meant that it was available only to those whose families could afford to pay tuition at private schools. Public elementary schools for girls began to open in the 1820s. In 1824, the first public high school for girls opened in Worcester, Massachusetts, but free public education at the high school level did not become available for girls, even in the larger cities, until after the Civil War.[35]

Colleges for men had existed for more than one hundred years, but at the beginning of the nineteenth century a college education was not available to women. When Oberlin College opened in 1833, it admitted women, but initially not to the regular course of study. Not until 1841 did a woman who had completed the full course of study available to men graduate from Oberlin.[36]

The efforts to establish women's rights focused on many different issues, but leaders of the women's suffrage movement believed that gaining the right to vote was the key to obtaining other rights more quickly, because by targeting their votes, they might bring effective pressure on legislators and executives to gain other rights.

The organized effort to obtain women's right to vote lasted from 1848 to 1920. Progress was slow, in part because dissension fragmented the women's suffrage movement into competing and contentious organizations during much of the struggle. Women's rights meetings were held at both the local and national levels. National women's rights conventions were held almost every year between 1850 and 1860. At these meetings, women voiced their dissatisfaction with their lack of rights; such discussions helped them clarify their beliefs about preferable solutions. The press eventually began to treat the meetings seriously; there was factual reporting but little editorial support. Dissatisfied with the coverage, some women founded and edited journals that included both factual information about women's issues and sympathetic views.

The absence of a permanent organization handicapped the women's movement in its early years. Women also lacked the strategic weapons they needed to increase support for their cause. All the major institutions of society—state and national legislatures, the courts, the political parties, the press, religious organizations—were arrayed against the women's movement.

One strategy that leaders of the women's movement did use with some effectiveness was to petition state legislatures for specific changes in laws. The goals of Susan B. Anthony's efforts to change New York State laws were to obtain for women: (1) the right to control their own earnings; (2) the right to obtain guardianship over their children in the event of divorce;

and (3) the right to vote. Her petition drive led to the establishment of county-level and, later, state-level women's organizations.[37]

Leaders of the women's suffrage movement expected that the granting of political and legal rights to blacks after the Civil War would be accompanied by the extension of those rights to women. However, Republican congressional leaders, fearing that the constitutional amendments would not be ratified by the states if those rights were extended to women, restricted the applicability of the Fourteenth and Fifteenth Amendments to black males. Greatly disappointed that women were not enfranchised by those amendments, in 1869 Elizabeth Cady Stanton and Susan B. Anthony established the National Woman Suffrage Association. The organization's goals were to obtain economic, social, political, and legal rights for women; one specific goal was the enactment of a constitutional amendment to enfranchise women. Believing that these goals were too broad and the strategy inappropriate, Lucy Stone in that year founded the American Woman Suffrage Association, which focused on the right to vote as the key to obtaining other policy changes, on the assumption that controversies associated with other goals could thus be avoided. The association also focused on obtaining the vote by means of state constitutional amendments rather than by a national constitutional amendment. These differences in goals and strategies divided the two organizations until 1890, when they merged to form the National American Woman Suffrage Association.

Several different interest groups opposed voting rights for women. Southern political leaders resented Northern women's support for the abolitionist movement prior to and during the Civil War. The patriarchal culture that prevailed among Southern political and social elites also contributed to Southern opposition to women's political and legal rights. Conservative religious leaders in both the Catholic Church and fundamentalist Protestant churches were opposed to women's suffrage. Some business interests were afraid that women's support for laws prohibiting children from working in factories would be more effective if women had the vote. Opposition also came from leaders of the corrupt political organizations that controlled some city and state governments. They believed that women would support political reforms designed to reduce the power of political bosses and would thus bring about more honest government and politics. Women's activism and leadership in the temperance movement caused brewery and liquor interests to fear that women's enfranchisement would result in the success of that movement. When Congress finally proposed the Nineteenth Amendment in June 1919 and sent it to the states for ratification, many changes opposed by these interests had already become law. Many states had enacted laws prohibiting children from working in the mines and factories and had instituted political reforms that restricted the power of political bosses. In January 1919, a constitutional amendment had been ratified that prohibited the manufacture, sale, and transportation of alcoholic beverages. Indeed, the suffrage movement received support from representatives of interests that believed women would support their goals with their votes.

Largely as a result of the skillful leadership of the women's suffrage movement provided by such women as Carrie Chapman Catt, who became president of the National American Woman Suffrage Association in 1915, both Democratic and Republican Parties included planks supporting (although with a weak commitment) women's suffrage in their platforms in 1916. Catt sought to win the support of President Woodrow Wilson for women's suffrage. The association's leaders strengthened both its state and its national organizations in pursuit of their goal—enactment of the women's suffrage amendment by Congress and ratification by the states. One wing of the movement emphasized a continuing campaign to inform and persuade political decision makers. Another organized silent picketing movements, protest marches, and other demonstrations to keep the issue before the American people and their political leaders. President Wilson endorsed the Nineteenth Amendment in January 1918, and it passed in the House of Representatives by a vote of 274 to 136. However, the Senate did not approve the amendment during that term of Congress; it lost by one vote. Not until 1919 did both the Senate and the House of Representatives vote in favor of the amendment. A spirited drive for ratification in the states followed, and Tennessee became the thirty-sixth state to ratify the amendment, on August 18, 1920.

Women in every state were now constitutionally guaranteed the most basic right—the right to vote. The campaign that had been sustained by the efforts of thousands of women in every state to educate and persuade, and to organize support for women's right to vote, had finally achieved its goal. The Nineteenth Amendment to the United States Constitution states:

> The right of citizens of the United States to vote shall not be denied or abridged by the United States or by any State on account of sex.
>
> Congress shall have the power to enforce this article by appropriate legislation.

The enactment of the Nineteenth Amendment was the beginning of a new chapter in the story of women's political participation. Since that time there have been radical changes in the way American women live their lives, as evidenced by the comparison of Eleanora and her daughters. Women have increasingly availed themselves of the opportunities presented in a liberal culture, and their gains have been accompanied by changes in women's political participation. American families and gender role expectations have changed, and this has resulted in increased options for women. Chapter 2 explores the effects of these and other cultural changes on women's political socialization and examines how the changes in political socialization have affected women.

NOTES

1. Eleanora Tomec was the mother of one of this book's coauthors.

2. Sara E. Rix, ed., for the Women's Research and Education Institute of the Congressional Caucus for Women's Issues, *The American Woman 1987–88: A Report in Depth* (New York: Norton, 1987), 292.

3. The divorce rate in 1945 was 3.5 divorces per 1,000 population. The marriage rate that year was 12.1 marriages per 1,000 population. U.S. Dept. of Commerce, Economics and Statistics Administration, Bureau of the Census, *Statistical Abstract of the United States, 1948* (Washington, D.C.: 1948), 89.

4. Ibid., 66.

5. Rix, *American Woman 1987–88*, 302.

6. U.S. Dept. of Commerce, Bureau of the Census, *Statistical Abstract of the United States, 1948*, 169.

7. Paula Ries and Anne J. Stone, eds., for the Women's Research and Education Institute of the Congressional Caucus for Women's Issues, *The American Woman 1992–93: A Status Report* (New York: Norton, 1992), 236.

8. Herbert M. Levine, *Political Issues Debate: An Introduction to Politics,* 4th ed. (Englewood Cliffs, N.J.: Prentice-Hall, 1993), 20.

9. This is the focus used in M. Margaret Conway, David Ahern, and Gertrude A. Steuernagel, *Women and Public Policy: A Revolution in Progress* (Washington, D.C.: CQ Press, 1994). See particularly the discussion of women, public policy, and culture in Chapter 1.

10. See, for example, John Rawls's widely acclaimed *A Theory of Justice* (Cambridge: Harvard University Press, 1971). According to a popular meaning of "liberal" today (not to be confused with the meaning used here), liberals are identified as supporters of big spending and big government but as opponents of family values.

11. M. Margaret Conway, *Political Participation in the United States,* 2d ed. (Washington, D.C.: CQ Press, 1991), 3–4.

12. Clearly, neither liberalism nor liberal culture is monolithic. There are groups that choose to live apart from the liberal culture (e.g., the Amish) and groups that, historically, have been denied the right to participate fully. Some observers have taken issue with the characterization of American culture as liberal. See, in particular, Richard M. Merelman, *Making Something of Ourselves: Our Culture and Politics in the United States* (Berkeley: University of California Press, 1984).

13. U.S. Dept. of Commerce, Economics and Statistics Administration, Bureau of the Census, *Statistical Abstract of the United States, 1995* (Washington, D.C.: 1995), 400.

14. Ries and Stone, *American Woman 1992–93,* 308, 321.

15. U.S. Dept. of Commerce, Bureau of the Census, *Statistical Abstract of the United States, 1995,* 406.

16. U.S. Dept. of Commerce, Bureau of the Census, *Statistical Abstract of the United States, 1948,* 169; *Statistical Abstract of the United States, 1995,* 412.

17. U.S. Dept. of Commerce, Bureau of the Census, *Statistical Abstract of the United States, 1995,* 411.

18. U.S. Dept. of Commerce, Economics and Statistics Administration, Bureau of the Census, *Statistical Abstract of the United States, 1951* (Washington, D.C.: 1951), 110.

19. Ries and Stone, *American Woman 1992–93,* 283, 289, 293.

20. See, for example, Theda Skocpol, *Protecting Soldiers and Mothers: The Political Origins of Social Policy in the United States* (Cambridge: Harvard University Press, Belknap Press, 1992).

21. Common law refers to that body of law arising from decisions made by judges in specific cases. This form of law developed before legislatures existed. It is contrasted with statute law, which refers to laws enacted by legislatures. See Judith A. Baer, *Women in American Law* (New York: Holmes and Meier, 1991), 14–15.

22. Earlean McCarrick, "Women and Family Law: Marriage and Divorce," in Conway, Ahern, and Steuernagel, *Women and Public Policy,* 125–126.

23. Eleanor Flexner, *Century of Struggle,* rev. ed. (Cambridge: Harvard University Press, Belknap Press, 1975), 15.

24. Ibid.

25. Ibid., 167.

26. Ibid., 179; Conway, *Political Participation,* 13–15; John J. Stucker, "Women as Voters: Their Maturation as Political Persons in American Society," in Marianne Githens and Jewel L. Prestage, *A Portrait of Marginality* (New York: McKay, 1977), Table 15.1, 267.

27. Stucker, "Women as Voters," Table 15.1, 267.

28. Ibid., Table 15.2, 269.

29. M. Margaret Conway, "Fostering Group-Based Political Participation," in Orit Ichilov, ed., *Political Socialization, Citizenship Education, and Democracy* (New York: Teacher's College Press, Columbia University, 1990), 297–312; Carole J. Uhlaner, "Rational Turnout: The Neglected Role of Groups," *American Journal of Political Science* 33 (1989): 390–422; Carole J. Uhlaner, "'Relational Goods' and Participation: Incorporating Sociability into a Theory of Rational Action," *Public Choice* 62 (1988): 253–285.

30. Flexner, *Century of Struggle,* 73–74.

31. Elizabeth Cady Stanton, Susan Anthony, and Mathilda Joselyn Gage, eds., *The History of Woman Suffrage* (Rochester, N.Y.: Susan B. Anthony and Charles Mann, 1881–1922), 1: 72.

32. Upon hearing the draft resolution concerning the vote, Stanton's husband informed her that he would leave town if that resolution were introduced at the convention. Flexner, *Century of Struggle,* 75.

33. Ibid., 77.

34. McCarrick, "Women and Family Law"; Dorothy McBride Stetson, *Women's Rights in the U.S.A.* (Pacific Grove, Calif.: Brooks/Cole, 1991), 138.

35. Flexner, *Century of Struggle,* 25–28.

36. Ibid., 29–30.

37. Ibid., 86. The remainder of this discussion draws on Chapters 10, 22, and 23 of Flexner.

SUGGESTIONS FOR FURTHER READING

Burr, Virginia Ingraham, ed. *The Secret Eye: The Journal of Ella Gertrude Clanton Thomas, 1848–1889.* Chapel Hill: University of North Carolina Press, 1990.

Carty, Linda, ed. *And Still We Rise: Feminist Political Mobilizing in Contemporary Canada.* Toronto: Women's Press, 1993.

Kelber, Mim, ed. *Women and Government: New Ways to Political Power.* Westport, Conn.: Greenwood Press, 1994.

Leonard, Elizabeth. *Yankee Women: Gender Battles in the Civil War.* New York: Norton, 1994.

Lerner, Gerda, ed. *Black Women in White America: A Documentary History.* New York: Vintage Books, 1972.

Rule, Wilma, and Joseph F. Zimmerman, eds. *Electoral Systems in Comparative Perspective.* Westport, Conn.: Greenwood Press, 1994.

Sigel, Roberta S. "How Men and Women Cope When Gender Role Orientations Change." *Political Psychology* 13 (3): 337–352.

CHAPTER 2

Women, Culture, and Political Socialization

Barbara Jordan was born in the segregated city of Houston, Texas, in 1936. From the beginning, family and friends recognized her abilities and urged her to set her sights beyond Houston.[1] Because she was the daughter of a minister, church and family were the foundations of her life. Because her skin was dark and she did not have "good hair," Jordan experienced discrimination on the part of some blacks, including teachers. Having watched her mother toil to provide for her family, Jordan knew she did not want to spend her life scrubbing floors, cooking, and washing clothes. She always knew she would go to college, and at some point during high school decided to become a lawyer. Her matriculation at Boston University Law School also marked her entry, for the first time, into the white world, where she was frequently treated as a black woman rather than as an individual. But Jordan learned to cope. She and other black students started their own study group when they were not invited to join any of the white study groups. She endured "Ladies Day," when she and the other usually ignored women in the law school class were actually called upon to participate. Jordan worked long hours; her segregated education had not adequately prepared her for the demands of law school. She was supported by her family, both emotionally and financially, and received her law degree in 1959. She returned to Houston, established a law practice, and became involved in John F. Kennedy's campaign for the presidency. Having been "bitten by the bug," she gained attention as a speaker at liberal Democratic gatherings.

Politics was attractive to Jordan in part because it was a way to do something to implement school desegregation. The case of *Brown v. Board of Education* (1954) had been all but ignored in Houston, and in 1962 the U.S. Court of Appeals, in *Ross v. Dyer,* ruled that the Houston school system was discriminating against black students.[2] The *Ross* case was a catalyst for Jordan's entry into politics. She developed some connections, and in 1962 entered her first race, for a seat in the Texas House of Representatives. But she lost that race, as well as her 1964 try for the same office. It was at this point that Jordan, who had always been ambivalent about marriage because it might confine her choices, decided that she could not have both marriage and a career in politics. She realized that public expectations were different for her as a black woman than they were for a white man. A man was perceived as being capable of combining marriage with a career in politics because his wife would take care of the domestic responsibilities. If she, as a black woman, were to defy expectations, she would have to make a choice; she chose politics over marriage. It was at this time that President Kennedy was assassinated, Lyndon Baines Johnson succeeded him, the Civil Rights Act of 1964 was passed, and the U.S. Supreme Court issued a series of reapportionment decisions.[3] Texas, like the rest of the country, was changing. In 1966, Barbara Jordan ran for a Senate seat and became the first black woman to be elected to the Texas legislature. She was aware that her race and gender might make some of her new colleagues uncomfortable and did her best to fit in. She made it clear, for example, that although she herself did not use profane language, she would not object if others used it in her presence. In 1968 she was reelected to the Texas Senate, and in 1972 was elected to the United States House of Representatives, securing a coveted seat on the Judiciary Committee. In 1974, when that committee began hearings on the impeachment of President Richard Nixon, her opening statement thrust her into the national spotlight. Her reputation was further enhanced by her articulate presentation as one of the keynote speakers at the 1976 Democratic National Convention.

Her supporters had hoped Jordan would be tapped as Jimmy Carter's running mate. When she was not, discussion centered on a cabinet post for her. From Jordan's perspective, it would have to be attorney general or nothing. But again she was passed over, and in 1976 she was reelected to her congressional seat.[4]

Jordan began to tire of the House and to think about a departure from politics. Eventually she decided not to seek a fourth term.

CULTURAL CHANGE AND GENDER ROLE EXPECTATIONS

A useful way to organize our thinking about the cultural changes whose impact has been experienced by Barbara Jordan and other women is to analyze what is known in the field of psychology as the "social clock": society's expectations, including those with regard to gender role, concerning appropriate behavior at different ages in life. All members of society are aware of these expectations. Society supports those who conform to this timetable and criticizes those who do not.[5] In 1950, a mother who worked outside the home when her children were very young would be contradicting the social clock. But should she decide to stay home and out of the paid work force until her youngest child graduated from high school, she would win approval for conforming to the social clock. If Barbara Jordan had been a man, her life would largely have been a model of compliance with the social clock. Her elementary and high school years were notable because of her many accolades and achievements. She went to college following high school and entered law school immediately after college. Jordan then began to build what would be a successful career in law and politics. Had she been a man, she would still have been expected, according to the social clock, to marry and father children. In this respect, she would not have conformed with the social clock; but since marriage and family were not considered as central to a man's existence as they were to a woman's, the disapproval might have been less severe than it was for Jordan as a woman. As a woman of color, however, she had a different social clock. She was expected to marry and have children and to make these the primary roles in her life. If she wanted a career (one that she would be expected to willingly interrupt during her children's younger years), the expectation was that she would choose the fields of education or social work. But Jordan chose politics, and in doing so she risked disapproval and ultimately incurred much of the negativity that accompanies nonconformance with the social clock. In this case, however, her rebellion came at a time when the culture was changing. The decade of the 1960s was characterized by tremendous social upheaval that gave rise to a number of movements for change, including the women's movement. For the individual willing to risk disapproval, as was Barbara Jordan, the opportunities were there. This change in the social clock is evident in the contrast between the life of Eleanora Tomec and the lives of her daughters.

Eleanora Tomec's life also reflected some contradictions of the social clock, but none were as radical as Barbara Jordan's. Eleanora delayed marriage and childbearing, but because World War II was a contributing factor, Eleanora did not receive the strong disapproval that would have been predicted by the social clock of her time. Another contradiction was that she went back to work while her children were small. But she returned to an appropriate profession, that of secretary, and she always placed her family's interests ahead of her work. She also worked to finance her children's education—a reason that was more acceptable at the time than reasons that would have been considered more selfish, such as advancement of her own career or the desire to achieve something for herself. According to the social clock, Eleanora's daughters were expected to pursue college educations, and they did. Although the younger daughter married relatively late in life, she was part of a continuing trend for professional women. The older daughter's divorce was not met with the disapproval that Eleanora might have experienced at the same age, for divorce is now accepted by society. The younger daughter's decision to remain in the work force during her child's preschool years was also not something that, according to the social clock of her time, would engender disapproval. Eleanora, her daughters, and Barbara Jordan lived their lives with an awareness of the social clocks of their time, and in living their lives they helped to change the gender role expectations established by the social clocks.

GENDER ROLE EXPECTATIONS AND POLITICAL SOCIALIZATION

Why did Barbara Jordan become a political activist? In what ways and to what extent did her family, church, schools, as well as the Democratic Party and the American culture as a whole shape her political attitudes? Such questions are the focus of the field of study known as political socialization. The study of political socialization is the study of political learning, which, like any kind of learning, continues throughout a person's life. Political socialization is the process by which people learn what is expected of them in their particular political system.[6]

Women's political socialization should be understood in the context of cultural expectations concerning appropriate gender role behavior. Despite the many changes in gender role expectations, there continue to be different expectations for men and women, and these translate into differences in political participation.

As girls, women learn to be more passive than boys and to care about things not commonly thought of as political. Furthermore, the socialization women experience as adults, in their family roles, has been thought to reinforce the idea that politics is not their business. Women have for so long been culturally restricted to the private world of home and family that when they enter the public world of politics, they face a struggle to be viewed as public figures, not private individuals.[7] Women's family responsibilities have been found to affect their political ambition and the kinds of political activism they pursue.[8] As the tie between women and the private world of home and family is lessened, politics is increasingly viewed as an appropriate area in which women can participate. Traditionally, women have not developed a sense of political efficacy, usually associated with political participation—that is, the sense that what a person does really matters. Women (as well as men) did not accept the idea that politics should be of concern to women. They did not run for political office because it was not considered "right," and party leaders as well as voters agreed. Women also had more domestic responsibilities, which affected the time they had to devote to politics. Even among political activists, women were more likely than men to curtail their political involvement to make time for family. When women did become involved in politics, their activity was likely to be related to their roles in the family, centering on local issues such as education.[9]

Cultural change has clearly had a direct impact on women's political participation. In general, the changes in gender role expectations have both reflected and given rise to changes in gender role socialization. These changes, in turn, affect how women perceive politics. Patterns of political participation change with changes in life experiences;[10] and cultural change in women's roles is required for women to become completely integrated into the world of politics.[11] Although women now vote in proportions equal to or greater than men, there are gender differences in political attitudes (see Chapter 3) and voting behavior (see Chapter 4). Moreover, there continue to be gender differences in rates of participation in areas other than voting. Women, for example, are less likely than men to be interested in politics or to engage in political discussions.[12] Overall, young men seem to be more politicized—that is, they have more of an awareness of politics and more motivation to participate—than young women.[13] Cultural change has made politics less a "man's thing," but differences in the way women and men live their lives continue to affect women's political behavior.

It is important to note, however, that the barriers to women's full participation in the nation's political affairs are not all attitudinal. Women still face constraints on their ability to participate politically. Many women are limited by situational factors, such as the demands of family life, and structural factors, such as lack of education, experience, and money.[14] Women are still less likely than men to be members of the legal profession, a career that is compatible with a career in politics (as in the case of Barbara Jordan). As more women enter the legal profession, more are likely to pursue leadership roles in politics. Cultural change has lessened the impact of situational and structural factors on women's political participation, but women's full participation in political affairs will occur only when men and women have the same degree of access to educational and employment opportunities.

CULTURAL CHANGE AND THE AGENTS OF SOCIALIZATION

Cultural change and political socialization are closely related.[15] Students of political socialization have always been concerned with agents of socialization, such as family, school, workplace, church, peer group, and the media.[16] Each of these agents has been shaped by the tremendous cultural changes that have occurred in the twentieth century, and they have also affected women's political socialization.

Family

The family, traditionally thought of as the primary agent of political socialization, is where children learn political attitudes and a basic orientation toward politics, particularly party identification. Attitudes toward both traditional and nontraditional forms of political activism are also thought to be transmitted in the family. Party activist parents, for example, are more likely to have children who become involved in party politics. Children of parents who were involved in political protests also seem to "inherit" their parents' inclination and are more likely to participate in such protests.[17]

The impact of cultural change on the family has been dramatic; gender role expectations have changed as women's roles in the family have changed. Polling data reveal that by the end of the 1980s, a majority of married women and men in the United States believed that the arrangement that worked best for them was one in which both spouses worked outside the home and shared domestic and child-rearing responsibilities. But as recently as the mid-1970s, a majority of both women and men wanted a marriage in which the husband was the financial provider and the wife cared for the children and the home.[18]

Marriage and family continue to be part of most women's lives, but women are now marrying later in life than women did in the 1970s. In 1970 the median age for women at the time of first marriage was 20.8 years. By 1992 this figure had increased to 24.4 years. Women are having fewer children than did women in the 1970s. They are also more likely than women were in the 1970s to be divorced and to be single parents.[19] In 1970 11.9 percent of children under the age of 18 lived with a single parent. By 1990, this percentage had increased to 24.7. In 1990, 54.8 percent of all black children lived with a single parent, compared with 31.8 percent in 1970.[20] Mothers and fathers alike are now coping with the demands of family and work, and young children are frequently cared for by people other than Mommy or Daddy.

School

Women in the 1990s are more likely to be high school graduates than women in the 1970s. They are also more likely to be enrolled in college; at all levels except the doctorate, there are more female than male degree recipients. This is not to say, however, that there has been a total change in gender role expectations. Although women are becoming more educated, they still tend to choose fields whose occupations are extensions of traditionally female roles such as early childhood education and nursing. They are less likely than men to major in disciplines such as computer science and engineering.[21]

Workplace

Women now constitute a greater proportion of the labor force than they did in 1970. Indeed, women's membership in the work force has steadily increased since the 1960s; more than half of all employed women are now full-time, year-round workers. The trend is particularly dramatic in the case of women with children under the age of 3. As noted in Chapter 1, more than half of the women with children under the age of 6 are now in the work force. In general, although more women are now working outside the home, women's choice of fields and occupations has not significantly changed. Although women are moving into traditional male fields such as medicine and law, there are still few women employed in skilled construction trades. Overall, women are concentrated in a narrower range of occupations than men; and these occupations, like women's choice of fields of study, tend to reflect traditional gender role expectations.[22]

Implications of Cultural Change
in Agents of Political Socialization

Changes in the agents of political socialization affect the direction of future changes in women's political participation. As more women become more educated, they are more likely to be interested in and to participate in politics, and to have a greater sense of their own political efficacy.[23] There is some evidence suggesting that in general, women who work outside the home have higher levels of political participation than women who are homemakers. Research also suggests that homemakers are less egalitarian in their beliefs than women in the work force. Moreover, women in the work force are more likely to try to persuade others how to vote, to attend political rallies, and to make campaign contributions.[24]

Adult socialization can occur in the workplace. This is significant because women continue to move into the labor force in unprecedented numbers. Socialization involves adapting to the environment, and this adaptation involves changes in attitudes.[25] (It is difficult to determine the exact nature of the process, however, because some self-selection takes place; women who enter the work force may have been different in the beginning from those who do not—for example, they may be more self-confident.) Evangelical women are a case in point. Evangelical women in the work force have more egalitarian attitudes concerning the role of women in politics and business than do evangelical homemakers, although both groups continue to hold traditional beliefs about their own roles as wives and mothers.[26]

These changes in life experience affect how women perceive themselves as women. Some women continue to define themselves in terms of traditional roles. Interestingly, women and men who continue to hold traditional views regarding women and politics are less likely to vote, less likely to be active in political campaigns and organizations concerned with national problems, and less likely to be politically active than those with more modern ideas.[27] It is also possible that women who experience the impact of these cultural changes, including changes in the traditional roles, will begin to see themselves not as isolated individuals but as members of a group with shared concerns. Gender consciousness, defined as "the recognition that one's relation to the political world is shaped in important ways by the physical fact of one's sex,"[28] will not lead all women to adopt the same political position, but it is necessary if women, who were once denied the opportunity of political participation because of their gender, are to understand that being female has political significance and to act accordingly. Not all women with gender consciousness support the women's movement, for example, but without gender consciousness women will not perceive themselves as a group with shared political interests. What is clear is that women's political participation increases as women's consciousness of themselves as a group increases.[29] (A more detailed discussion of the implications of the development of gender consciousness is included in Chapter 3.)

The women's movement has contributed to the effort to help women develop gender consciousness. The National Organization for Women has successfully worked for the passage of legislation in areas such as credit, sexual harassment, and health care. Its members believe that the policies they support not only improve women's lives but help to empower women by making them more aware of the experiences and needs they share as women—an important step in the development of gender consciousness among women.[30]

Not all women share the same experiences, however, and this can affect the development of gender consciousness. For some women, race or religion may be more important politically than gender; for others, their economic situation may be the factor that is most politically relevant.[31] Economically, women are clearly not a monolithic group. In 1994, for example, 3.4 percent of the white married couples without children lived in poverty. In contrast, 60.5 percent of the families headed by black females with children lived in poverty.[32] In general, women earn less than men, but the picture is complicated by such factors as race and ethnic origin. White men earn more than white women; black men earn more than black women; and Hispanic men earn more than Hispanic women. White women earn more than Hispanic men, and the earnings of white women and black men are approximately equal.[33]

Age also affects the development of gender consciousness. The period in which a woman is born and her age at the time of significant societal change tend to shape her political beliefs.[34] Baby boomers, those born between 1946 and 1964, are the group commonly thought to be most affected by the women's movement and by public policies such as Title IX of the Higher Education Act Amendments (which prohibited sexual discrimination by educational institutions). But there are generational differences even among baby boomers. A girl born in 1946 would have been 26 years old at the time of the enactment of Title IX. But a girl born in 1964 would have been 8 years old; she would be young enough to avail herself of the opportunities afforded her by Title IX, but she might assume that they had always been available to women.

There is some indication that support for feminism will increase among women as more of them experience the impact of changes in the traditional roles of wife and mother.[35] It is also possible that women will increasingly identify psychologically with one another even though they differ in terms of class, race, and age.[36] As women continue to share experiences at home, school, and work, these psychological bonds may contribute to the development of gender consciousness.

IT'S A MAN'S WORLD, BUT TIMES ARE CHANGING

In analyzing the consequences of cultural change for agents of political socialization as they affect both women and political participation, it is helpful to think of women's increased political involvement in terms of acculturation, the process by which one group becomes integrated into the way of life of another group. Immigrants have traditionally become acculturated to the way of living of their adopted homeland, but acculturation can take a variety of forms. As discussed in Chapter 1, Eleanora's parents wanted her to be an American. For them, this meant that Eleanora was to speak, dress, and conduct herself as an American. Their own acculturation was less complete. They learned to speak English, but they frequently spoke their native Slovenian to each other. Although Eleanora's mother continued to cook and bake Slovenian dishes, she never taught her daughter how to prepare them but rather insisted that because American men liked

American food, Eleanora should learn how to prepare hamburgers and hot dogs. What Eleanora's parents seemed not to understand was that acculturation, particularly in the United States, is seldom linear. Immigrants have reshaped American culture in the process of joining it. Eleanora's mother's strudel is therefore as American as apple pie.

As women become more involved in politics, they become more acculturated. Given the history of male domination of political affairs in the United States, women's increased participation in politics is comparable to a wave of immigration. Barbara Jordan attempted to fit in with other members of the Texas state legislature. One indication of male domination of political affairs is the number of sports and military metaphors that are frequently employed in speaking and writing about politics. A campaign is a "run" for political office. The leading candidate is the front runner and an unknown is a dark horse. A pollster frequently uses a "horse race question." A candidate who is hurt by an opponent's attack may be "down for the count." The candidate who does not foresee an opponent's strategy may be "ambushed." Some candidates choose to run a "stealth" campaign and to "hunker down" or "stay in the bunkers" to avoid engagement with their opponents. This gives them time to "circle the wagons" and orchestrate a defense against the opponents' attacks. Election day volunteers involved in get-out-the-vote activities are known as "foot soldiers." Other volunteers may call upon "targets," or selected voters.

If women are to become fully integrated into politics, a certain amount of acculturation must occur; women need to think of themselves as public figures as well as private individuals. As increasing numbers of women participate politically, they are changing the culture of politics. One study found female state legislators to be more supportive than their male colleagues of conducting governmental business in public view rather than behind closed doors. The same study revealed that female state legislators were more likely than their male colleagues to bring citizens into the policy-making process.[37] Changes are also being observed in the political agenda. An issue such as child care is now considered an appropriate item for the political agenda rather than strictly a private matter. In addition, some candidates for political office, cognizant of the gender gap in voting, take care to promote themselves as the "environmental governor" or the "education president." Even Congress, one of the most traditional and most male-dominated political institutions, made its gymnasium facilities available to female members.[38] Like the acculturation of immigrant groups, however, the political integration of women is affected by a num-

ber of factors, such as the perception of a woman's capabilities and qualifications. Much of what immigrants do in adapting to the political culture
of their new country is a function of that country's attitudes toward them.
In receptive host countries, immigrants are likely to attempt to unlearn
their old political attitudes, a process known as desocialization, and to learn
new ones that are appropriate to their new homeland, a process known as
resocialization. When the host country is not particularly receptive, however, immigrants may adopt some of the new attitudes but they usually do
not desocialize or resocialize.[39] To a large extent, then, the future of
women's political participation depends on the receptivity of what has
been a male-oriented political culture.

NOTES

1. All of the information concerning Barbara Jordan is from Barbara Jordan
and Shelby Hearon, *Barbara Jordan: A Self-Portrait* (Garden City, N.Y.: Doubleday,
1979). Barbara Jordan died in 1996. President Bill Clinton spoke at her funeral.

2. *Brown v. Board of Education*, 347 U.S. 483 (1954); *Ross v. Dyer*, 312 F. 2d 191
(5th Cir. 1962).

3. *Baker v. Carr*, 369 U.S. 186 (1962); *Reynolds v. Sims*, 377 U.S. 533 (1963);
Wesberry v. Sanders, 376 U.S. 1 (1964).

4. Not until the election of Bill Clinton would there be a female attorney
general—Janet Reno. When Clinton was reelected in 1996, one of his first
appointments was Madeleine K. Albright, who was confirmed as the first female
secretary of state. A woman has not yet held either of the two other major cabinet posts—secretary of defense and Treasury secretary.

5. Irene H. Frieze, Jacquelynne E. Parsons, Paula B. Johnson, Diane N. Ruble,
and Gail L. Zellman, *Women and Sex Roles: A Social Psychological Perspective* (New
York: Norton, 1978), 163–164.

6. For a general discussion of political socialization, including its "ups and
downs," see Pamela Johnston Conover, "Political Socialization: Where's the
Politics?" in William Crotty, ed., *Political Science: Looking to the Future*, vol. 3,
Political Behavior (Evanston, Ill.: Northwestern University Press, 1991), 125–152.

7. Virginia Sapiro, *The Political Integration of Women: Roles, Socialization, and
Politics* (Urbana: University of Illinois Press, 1983), chap. 2.

8. Virginia Sapiro and Barbara Farah, "New Pride and Old Prejudice: Political
Ambition and Role Orientations among Female Partisan Elites," *Women and
Politics* 1, no. 1 (spring 1980): 13–36.

9. For a discussion of women running for political office, see Susan J. Carroll,
Women as Candidates in American Politics, 2d ed. (Bloomington: Indiana University

Press, 1994), 310–323; and Virginia Sapiro, "Private Costs of Public Commitments or Public Costs of Private Commitments? Family Roles Versus Political Ambition," *American Journal of Political Science* 26, no. 2 (May 1982): 265–279.

10. M. Margaret Conway, *Political Participation in the United States,* 2d ed. (Washington, D.C.: CQ Press, 1991), 29.

11. Sapiro, *Political Integration of Women,* 27.

12. Gertrude A. Steuernagel, Thom Yantek, and Irene Barnett, "More Than Pink and Blue: Gender, Occupational Stratification, and Political Attitudes," in Lois Lovelace Duke, ed., *Women in Politics: Outsiders or Insiders?* 2d ed. (Chicago: Prentice Hall, 1996).

13. Diana Owen and Jack Dennis, "Sex Differences in Politicization: The Influence of Mass Media," *Women and Politics* 12, no. 4 (1992): 19–41. See also Diana Owen and Jack Dennis, "Gender Differences in the Politicization of American Children," *Women and Politics* 8, no. 2 (1988): 23–43.

14. Much of the research, particularly the early work, on women and political participation has focused on the relative effects of socialization and situational and structural factors. See Cal Clark and Janet Clark, "Models of Gender and Political Participation in the United States," *Women and Politics* 6, no. 1 (spring 1986): 5–25; Susan C. Bourque and Jean Grossholtz, "Politics and Unnatural Practice: Political Science Looks at Female Participation," *Politics and Society* 2, no. 4 (1974): 225–266; Susan B. Hansen, Linda M. Franz, and Margaret Netemeyer-Mays, "Women's Political Participation and Policy Preferences," *Social Science Quarterly* 56, no. 4 (March 1976): 576–590; Fred I. Greenstein, "Sex-Related Political Differences in Childhood," *Journal of Politics* 23, no. 2 (May 1961): 353–371; Kent L. Tedin, David W. Brady, and Arnold Vedlitz, "Sex Differences in Political Attitudes: The Case for Situational Factors," *Journal of Politics* 39, no. 2 (May 1977): 448–456; Kristi Andersen, "Working Women and Political Participation: 1952–1972," *American Journal of Political Science* 19, no. 3 (August 1975): 439–453; Susan Welch, "Women as Political Animals? A Test of Some Explanations for Male-Female Political Participation Differences," *American Journal of Political Science* 21, no. 4 (November 1977): 711–730; Anthony M. Orum, Roberta S. Cohen, Sherri Grasmuck, and Amy W. Orum, "Sex, Socialization, and Politics," *American Sociological Review* 39, no. 2 (April 1974): 197–209; Susan Gluck Mezey, "Does Sex Make a Difference? A Case Study of Women in Politics," *Western Political Quarterly* 31, no. 4 (December 1978): 493–501; Fred I. Greenstein, *Children and Politics* (New Haven: Yale University Press, 1969).

15. For a more detailed discussion of theories about women and political socialization, see Clark and Clark, "Gender and Political Participation," 5–25.

16. Those interested in comparative politics should see, for example, Michael H. Banks and Debra Roker, "The Political Socialization of Youth: Exploring the Influence of School Experience," *Journal of Adolescence* 17 (1994): 3–15, for a discussion of political socialization in England. Also useful is Anders Westholm and

Richard G. Niemi, "Political Institutions and Political Socialization: A Cross-National Study," *Comparative Politics* 25, no. 1 (October 1992): 25–41.

17. Darren E. Sherkat and T. Jean Blocker, "The Political Development of the Sixties' Activists: Identifying the Influence of Class, Gender, and Socialization on Protest Participation," *Social Forces* 72, no. 3 (March 1994): 821–842.

18. Cited in Nancy E. McGlen and Karen O'Connor, *Women, Politics, and American Society* (Englewood Cliffs, N.J.: Prentice-Hall, 1995), 250.

19. Cynthia Costello and Anne J. Stone, eds., for the Women's Research and Education Institute of the Congressional Caucus for Women's Issues, *The American Woman 1994–95: Where We Stand* (New York: Norton, 1994), 256, 258, 259, 261.

20. Paula Ries and Anne J. Stone, eds., for the Women's Research and Education Institute of the Congressional Caucus for Women's Issues, *American Woman 1992–93: A Status Report* (New York: Norton, 1992), 256.

21. Costello and Stone, *The American Woman 1994–95,* 268, 271–275.

22. Ibid., 282, 283, 291, 298.

23. Carroll, *Women as Candidates,* 323.

24. Kristi Andersen and Elizabeth A. Cook, "Women, Work, and Political Attitudes," *American Journal of Political Science* 29, no. 3 (August 1985): 613.

25. Ibid., 606–625.

26. Clyde Wilcox, "Evangelicalism, Social Identity, and Gender Attitudes among Women," *American Politics Quarterly* 19, no. 3 (July 1991): 353–363.

27. Linda L. M. Bennett and Stephen E. Bennett, "Changing Views About Gender Equality in Politics: Gradual Change and Lingering Doubts," in Duke, *Women in Politics,* 46–66.

28. Sue Tolleson-Rinehart, *Gender Consciousness and Politics* (New York: Routledge, 1992), 14.

29. Arthur H. Miller, Patricia Gurin, Gerald Gurin, and Oksana Malanchuk, "Group Consciousness and Political Participation," *American Journal of Political Science* 25, no. 3 (August 1981): 494–511.

30. Ethel Klein, *Gender Politics* (Cambridge: Harvard University Press, 1984), 3.

31. Melanie McCoy, "Gender or Ethnicity: What Makes a Difference? A Study of Women Tribal Leaders," *Women and Politics* 12, no. 3 (1992): 57–68.

32. Costello and Stone, *The American Woman 1994–95,* 337.

33. Ibid., 314.

34. Paul Allen Beck and M. Kent Jennings, "Family Traditions, Political Periods, and the Development of Partisan Orientations," *Journal of Politics* 53, no. 3 (August 1991): 743.

35. Klein, *Gender Politics,* 165. See also McGlen and O'Connor, *Women, Politics, and American Society,* 305.

36. Jeffrey W. Kock, "Is Group Membership a Prerequisite for Group Identification?" *Political Behavior* 15, no. 1 (March 1993): 49–60.

37. Susan J. Carroll, Debra L. Dodson, and Ruth B. Mandel, *The Impact of*

Women in Public Office: An Overview (New Brunswick, N.J.: Center for the American Woman and Politics, Eagleton Institute of Politics, Rutgers University, 1991), 23.

38. Male-dominated political institutions do not readily change without a little help. Concerning the integration of the gymnasium of the House of Representatives, see Barbara Boxer and Nicole Boxer, *Strangers in the Senate: Politics and the New Revolution of Women in America* (Washington, D.C.: National Press Books, 1993), 109–112.

39. For a fuller discussion, see Marilyn Hoskin, "Socialization and Anti-Socialization: The Case of Immigrants," in Roberta S. Sigel, ed., *Political Learning in Adulthood: A Sourcebook of Theory and Research* (Chicago: University of Chicago Press, 1989), 340–377.

SUGGESTIONS FOR FURTHER READING

Cohen, Margaret. "The Most Suffering Class: Gender, Class, and Consciousness in Pre-Marxist France." *Boundary 2* 18, no. 2 (summer 1991): 22–46.

Coles, Robert. *The Political Life of Children.* Boston: Atlantic Monthly Press, 1986.

Collins, Patricia Hill. *Black Feminist Thought: Knowledge, Consciousness, and the Politics of Empowerment.* New York: Routledge, 1991.

Cook, Elizabeth Adell. "Measuring Feminist Consciousness." *Women and Politics* 9, no. 3 (fall 1989): 71–88.

Davis, Nancy J. "Men's and Women's Consciousness of Gender Inequality: Austria, West Germany, Great Britain, and the United States." *American Sociological Review* 56, no. 1 (February 1991): 72–84.

Groth, Alexander J., and Charles R. Dannehl, "Women in Higher Education: Economic, Political, and Cultural Influences." *Women and Politics* 12, no. 1 (spring 1992): 53–69.

Held, Virginia. *Feminist Morality: Transforming Culture, Society, and Politics.* Chicago: University of Chicago Press, 1993.

Hunt, Pauline. *Gender and Class Consciousness.* New York: Holmes and Meier, 1980.

Young, Iris Marion. "Gender as Seriality: Thinking about Women as a Social Collective." *Signs* 19, no. 3 (spring 1994): 713–738.

CHAPTER 3

Gender Differences in Political Attitudes, Beliefs, and Policy Preferences

Jim and Sue are happily married. They believe their marital tranquility is best preserved by not discussing certain issues about which they strongly disagree. One such issue is gun control. Sue opposes individual ownership of handguns. Jim believes that every citizen should have the right to own however many guns of whatever type he or she wants to own. Another issue they avoid is affirmative action policy. Having been discriminated against both before she was hired for a job and before she obtained a much desired promotion in the company where she now works, Sue supports the government's vigorous enforcement of affirmative action policies that require nondiscrimination in employment practices. Having been passed over in favor of a woman for a promotion in his company that Jim believes he merited, he opposes affirmative action policies.

Such policy disagreements raise the questions that are addressed in this chapter: Do men and women differ in their policy preferences, perceptions of candidates and parties, and beliefs about the political system? Do women differ among themselves in their policy preferences? If so, to what extent? What are the possible explanations for the existence of gender differences in political orientation and political participation? The term "gender gap" refers to differences between men and women in their political attitudes, beliefs, values, policy preferences, issue agendas, political party affiliations, and vote choices. If a gender gap exists, it may significantly affect electoral outcomes and the public policies that elected and appointed officials create, amend, implement, enforce, and adjudicate. Journalists, politicians, and scholars continue to debate whether and to what extent a gender gap exists in political orientation and behavior, the reasons for its existence, and its consequences for politics and public policy.

In this chapter, "political orientation" refers to political beliefs, attitudes, and values, and their expression through various types of political action. Differences in political orientation can be viewed in two ways: as gender differences in political attitudes, beliefs, and values, and as gender role differences. Gender roles, which are created by the culture and learned by individuals, are expectations about how individuals should behave; they have implications for attitudes, beliefs, and values that pertain to politics. In this chapter we will examine differences in political attitudes, beliefs, policy preferences, and candidate evaluations both between women and men and among women who have different gender role perspectives.

As discussed in Chapter 2, gender consciousness as it relates to political behavior is "the recognition that one's relation to the political world is shaped in important ways by the physical fact of one's sex."[1] Elements of gender consciousness include identification with other group members, positive feelings toward other group members, perceptions of group advantage or disadvantage relative to other groups, and a sense of collective destiny.[2] Women group members who have gender consciousness may differ in their political orientation and political activity from those who do not.

POSSIBLE EXPLANATIONS FOR GENDER DIFFERENCES IN POLITICAL ORIENTATION

Theories are devices for selective perception that suggest what to look for, how the things perceived are related, what affects them, and possible consequences of the patterns found. Some scholars have criticized research on differences in men's and women's political orientation and political participation because the theories used to guide that research ignore the impact of gender roles. Certainly the theories used to study social phenomena affect the conclusions drawn, and such theories often ignore the effect of gender differences on individual and group processes and behavior.

Why might the gender roles learned by men and women result in differences in their political orientation? One possible explanation is differences in children's political socialization—that is, males and females learn different orientations with regard to politics. Children are taught social roles that are deemed appropriate by agents of socialization such as parents, teachers, religious leaders, social group leaders, and the mass media. Certain attitudes, beliefs, values, and behaviors are associated with those roles. Learning of social roles can be either direct or indirect (see Chapter 2). Prior to the 1960s, when the modern women's movement began to gain prominence, significant gender-related differences existed among children; girls were less interested in politics, had less political knowledge, and perceived those who wielded political authority such as the president and the police as benevolent figures.[3] Studies conducted in the 1960s and 1970s revealed that boys and girls continued to differ in some measures of political orientation. Cultural lags may exist because of the socialization of younger citizens by adults who were themselves socialized in a patriarchal society.[4]

More recent research suggests that gender differences in childhood learning about politics remain, but have diminished over time. A 1985 study of students aged 10 to 17 found significant differences between males and females in approximately half the measures of politicization.[5] In another study, individuals were surveyed as high school seniors in 1972 and again in 1974 after their graduation; females were found to have been more active in high school activities than males and more likely to believe in the value of the democratic process. However, when surveyed in 1976 and 1986, those females were found less likely to be active in politics than their male former classmates.[6] There are also generational differences, suggesting that women's support for feminist policies has changed over time. A 1970 comparison of mothers and daughters indicated that daughters were more supportive of a feminist agenda than were their mothers.[7]

A second possible explanation for continuing gender differences in political orientation is the differential treatment of men and women in the framing and interpretation of laws and of government rules and regulations. Although many overt forms of sexual discrimination in employment, access to housing, and educational opportunities were made illegal by federal and state antidiscrimination and affirmative action laws enacted in the 1960s and 1970s, subtle forms of discrimination still exist. Adult learning of the implications of gender roles—for example, an increased awareness of differential treatment by employers and of restricted employment opportunities (the "glass ceiling," which limits the promotion of women to senior management positions)—may influence some women's political orientation. The result of this learning process may be differences in political attitudes, beliefs, and values, both between men and women and among women.[8]

Early gender role socialization may reinforce the perception of existing structured inequalities in educational attainment, occupation, and income. Women tend to have lower levels of educational attainment and fewer occupational opportunities. Differences in cultural orientation may also affect the political orientation of women.[9]

Religious beliefs affect political orientation—a third possible explanation of gender differences. The doctrines of many religions are based on patriarchal authority, although the degree to which women are proscribed from engaging in political activity varies. Women who are members of denominations that adopt a patriarchal view of roles appropriate for women would be expected to be less supportive of gender equality in government, business, and society. Evangelical women have been found to be less supportive of equal rights for women than nonevangelical women. Adherence to evangelical doctrine is also associated with opposition to abortion and decreased support for the women's movement as well as decreased support for government assistance to improve the socioeconomic status of women.[10] Although evangelical women as a group tend to be more conservative on women's issues, a substantial proportion are supportive of moderate positions.[11] Two-fifths believe that women should have an equal role with men, one-third support federal government efforts to improve the socioeconomic status of women, and one-sixth support abortion rights.[12]

GENDER DIFFERENCES IN POLITICAL ATTITUDES AND BELIEFS

Women and men differ with regard to a number of political attitudes and beliefs. They have different views on several policy issues that relate to what can be labeled compassion for others. Women are more supportive of the view that government should provide services and assistance to those who are less fortunate. Women and men also differ on issues relating to the use of force; women are more likely to support gun control, to oppose the use of force to resolve conflicts, and to support decreased government funding for military programs. Women and men differ in their views on affirmative action and sexual harassment issues and in their support for government efforts to deal with these problems. Men tend to be more politically knowledgeable than women, particularly with regard to the federal government and national politics. Women are more likely to identify with the Democratic Party and to support Democratic candidates; men tend to identify with the Republican Party. But few gender differences exist in attitudes and beliefs on several policy issues. These include trustworthiness and effectiveness of the federal government and abortion policy.

GENDER DIFFERENCES IN PUBLIC POLICY PREFERENCES

Many organizations sponsor surveys that facilitate an examination of change in Americans' political orientations over time. The annual survey of the National Opinion Research Center of the University of Chicago and the biennial survey of the Center for Political Studies of the University of Michigan include a number of relevant items that have the same wording; thus they permit the analysis of change over time in patterns of men's and women's views on a number of policy issues as well as their political orientation.

Opinions on Policy Issues

EXPANSION OF GOVERNMENT PROGRAMS AND SERVICES. One indicator of policy preferences is the level of support for increased governmental spending for a particular program or service. In a national study conducted in 1992, a representative sample of the American electorate was asked several questions designed to measure support for several types of public policies. The survey respondents were requested to place themselves on a seven-point continuum, ranging from strong support (for more spending and services) to strong opposition. One item was worded as follows:

> Some people think the government should provide fewer services, even in areas such as health and education, in order to reduce spending. Suppose these people are at one end at point one. Other people feel it is important for the government to provide services even if it means an increase in spending. Suppose these people are at the other end at point 7. And of course, some other people have opinions somewhere in between at points 2, 3, 4, 5, or 6. Where would you place yourself on this scale, or haven't you thought much about this?[13]

If those who support an increase (points 5, 6, and 7) are placed in one category and those who oppose an increase (points 1, 2, and 3) are placed in another, men and women are found to differ significantly on issues of government spending as measured by this scale. Forty-two percent of the women compared with 32 percent of the men supported provision of more services and increased spending in policy areas such as health and education; only 26 percent of the women, compared with 38 percent of the men, supported decreased spending. Similar but weaker patterns are found when the issue is health insurance; a majority (54 percent) of the women supported a government health insurance plan, compared with 48 percent of the men. In contrast, 32 percent of the men and 24 percent of the women supported payment of all health costs by individuals and through private health insurance plans. However, when the issue is defense spending, a plurality of both men and women surveyed preferred to spend much less money; only 20 percent of the men and 18 percent of the women endorse greatly increased defense spending.[14] But when respondents were asked whether military strength should be maintained even if it would require continued high defense spending, women were found to be significantly less likely than men to support such an expenditure.[15]

Another way to measure support for various public policies is to ask whether governmental spending for a particular program should be increased or decreased, or whether it should remain the same. Women were significantly more willing than men to increase spending for financial aid for college students, the homeless problem, aid to the poor, child care programs, crime prevention, environmental improvement, social security programs, and public schools. Women were less willing than men to decrease spending on welfare and urban assistance programs, but more willing to decrease foreign aid to the new countries that were part of the Soviet Union. Men were more supportive than women of increased federal spending for science and technology.[16]

USE OF FORCE TO SOLVE PROBLEMS. Women and men differ in their readiness to approve of the use of force, as indicated by their responses on a variety of policy issues ranging from the death penalty to gun control to the use of U.S. troops to protect national security interests abroad. Women are consistently less supportive of the death penalty for persons convicted of crimes such as murder and more supportive of restrictions on possession of handguns.[17] Since the 1940s, women have been less supportive of the use of force to maintain peace and stability abroad and more supportive of negotiated settlements.[18]

ABORTION POLICY. A number of surveys have examined Americans' preferences on abortion policy. The questions asked by different survey organizations vary in their wording, and some survey organizations have also changed the wording of their abortion policy questions over time. Because small differences in the wording of questions on a particular policy issue can result in significant variations in response patterns, an analysis of changes in opinion on abortion policy over time must be limited to comparing responses to the same question asked at different points in time. The National Opinion Research Center of the University of Chicago has used the same wording over time in its annual General Social Survey. The Center for Political Studies of the University of Michigan, in its biennial American National Election Study, used two different wordings in 1972–1980 and in 1980–1994, so comparisons can also be made for each of those two periods.

Analysis of data from the General Social Survey indicates that since the mid-1980s, there has consistently been strong public support for legalized abortion when the woman's health would be seriously threatened by continuation of the pregnancy, when a serious defect exists in the fetus, or when pregnancy occurred as a consequence of rape or incest. The public has been much less supportive of abortion for more social reasons, such as when the woman is married and does not want more children, or the family has a very low income and cannot afford to support any more children, or the woman is not married and does not want to marry the father. (In one study, the first three circumstances are referred to as "traumatic abortion" and the last three as "elective abortion," respectively. Since the 1970s, public support has been much higher for traumatic abortions than for elective abortions.[19]) Women are slightly less supportive of abortion than men, but the differences are very small. Only among the oldest age groups (65 years and older) are the differences between men and women significant.[20]

Because the wording of the abortion attitude item in the American National Election Study survey changed between 1980 and 1984, it is somewhat difficult to examine changes in attitudes from 1972 to 1994. However, gender comparisons on this issue can still be made for each year and for a limited range of years. Tables 3-1 and 3-2 indicate the patterns of responses to the question of under what circumstances, if any, abortion

TABLE 3-1

Gender Differences in Opinion on the Abortion Issue, 1972–1980 (percent)

Opinion	1972		1976[a]		1980[a]	
	Men	Women	Men	Women	Men	Women
Should never be permitted	10	12	11	11	9	10
Permit only when life and health of the woman is endangered	45	48	42	48	45	44
Permit if woman would have difficulty in caring for the child	18	17	18	16	21	16
Should never be forbidden	26	23	30	25	25	30

Sources: Calculated from data in the 1952–1990 American National Election Studies Cumulative File.

[a] $p < .05$.

should be permitted. Three conclusions can be drawn from these data. First, men and women do not differ substantially in their views on this issue. Second, abortion appears to be viewed increasingly as a matter of personal choice. Approximately 10 percent of the men and 12 percent to 14 percent of the women surveyed since 1980 have been opposed to abortion under any circumstances. But since 1980 an increasing majority of both men and women have supported allowing abortion as a matter of personal choice; that was the policy preference of 41 percent of the men and 45 percent of the women surveyed in 1994. Third, question wording does matter. In 1980, when both question wordings were presented to the same interviewees, more were found to be pro-choice when the most pro-choice response was stated as "a matter of personal choice" than when the wording of that response was "should never be forbidden."

In 1992, national surveys asked respondents if they would favor or oppose a state law requiring parental consent before a minor (under age 18) could have an abortion; 78 percent of the men and 74 percent of the women said they favored such a law. But 48 percent of the men and 51 percent of the women opposed the use of government funding to pay for abortions; 71 percent of the men and 61 percent of the women favored requiring a married woman to obtain her husband's permission before she could have an abortion.[21]

Attitudes toward abortion policy are related to political ideology and

TABLE 3-2

Gender Differences in Opinion on the Abortion Issue, 1980–1994 (percent)

Opinion	1980 Men	1980 Women	1984 Men	1984 Women	1988[a] Men	1988[a] Women	1992 Men	1992 Women	1994 Men	1994 Women
Should never be permitted	11	12	12	14	10	14	9	12	10	14
Permit only in case of rape or incest or to save the life of the woman	32	33	28	32	33	33	28	28	33	29
Permit for other reasons, but only after need has been established	22	17	22	19	20	17	16	13	16	12
Matter of personal choice	36	37	38	35	36	35	47	47	41	45

Source: Calculated from data in the 1952–1990 American National Election Studies Cumulative File and the 1992 American National Election Study.

[a] p < .05.

level of educational attainment. Those who are more conservative tend to be less supportive of abortion. Level of educational attainment is the stronger predictor of attitudes toward abortion, however; those with less education are more strongly opposed to abortion.[22] One explanation is that higher levels of education increase tolerance for the differing views.

AFFIRMATIVE ACTION. Prior to passage of the Civil Rights Act of 1964, discrimination based on sex, race, or other sociodemographic characteristics in hiring, promotion, distribution of benefits, and other conditions of employment was not only legal but was widely practiced in the United States. Title VII of the Civil Rights Act of 1964 prohibits discrimination in employment on the basis of a number of sociodemographic characteristics, including sex.[23] In 1972 Congress extended the coverage of this law to include educational institutions. Also in 1972, Title IX of the Higher Education Act Amendments extended the prohibition against sexual discrimination in education to cover admissions and other aspects of educational programs.[24] At first, enforcement of these civil rights laws was passive, occurring only after a violation was reported to the enforcing agency, but during the late 1970s the enforcement focus began to shift to the initiation of affirmative action.[25] Affirmative action programs emphasize an open recruitment process, establishment of training and skills development programs for all employees, and promotion criteria that are based on employees' ability and performance, not on their race, sex, or other sociodemographic characteristics. Courts may impose quotas for hiring and require balanced promotion programs to overcome past patterns of discrimination. The necessity and fairness of affirmative action programs are often subjects of controversy.[26]

Efforts to determine the extent to which the public supports affirmative action suggest that question wording has a significant influence on the patterns of support or opposition. Some surveys indicate that a substantial proportion of the public may oppose hiring less-qualified individuals on the basis of their race or sex, giving preference in admissions to educational programs to minorities, and setting aside a proportion of government contracts for minority-owned firms. When asked whether they favored "requiring employers to actively seek out qualified minority and women applicants for jobs," 54 percent of the respondents in one study said they opposed that action. When asked if special consideration should be given to women, to increase their opportunities for admission to college or for jobs and promotions, only 33 percent said they favored such special considerations.[27] In another survey, subjects were asked whether giving preference to women in hiring or promotion results in discrimination against men; 52 percent responded in the affirmative.[28] The question in yet another study was worded differently; when respondents were asked if they strongly favored, favored, strongly opposed, or somewhat opposed giving preference to female job applicants who were equally as qualified as male applicants, 59 percent said they somewhat favored or strongly favored giving preference in hiring to female job applicants.[29] Support for affirmative action appears to vary with the context. Affirmative action for women appears to elicit more support than affirmative action that focuses on both minorities and women.

Opposition to giving special consideration to women in education and employment can be explained in part by the public's perception that things are much better or somewhat better for women than they were twenty-five years ago. In a 1992 survey, only 6 percent of the respondents said they thought women's opportunities were worse than they were twenty-five years ago; 79 percent said they thought opportunities were somewhat better or much better.[30] However, in a 1994 survey, women were found to be slightly less likely than men to believe that women have an equal chance to succeed (59 percent of the women respondents, compared with 64 percent of the men).[31] In another national survey carried out in 1995, women were asked if they had ever been discriminated against by not being offered a job; 19 percent of them responded yes, and 13 percent of the women said they had been discriminated against in promotions.[32]

Among men, support for affirmative action programs for women varies by age cohort. Younger men, aged 18 to 29 (55 percent), and those in the 45 to 64 age group (59 percent) are most likely to favor affirmative action programs for women (see Table 3-3). Women are much more supportive of affirmative action programs for women than are men in the same age group. For example, 73 percent of the women in the 18 to 29 age group support affirmative action programs for women, compared with 55 percent of the men. Among women, the support is least strong among those aged 30 to 44; only 63 percent support affirmative action programs for women and 24 percent are opposed. Among men in that age group, 48 percent support affirmative action for women and 35 percent oppose it. In the other two age groups (ages 45 to 64 and age 65 and over), 75 percent and 71 percent of the women, respectively, support affirmative action programs for women, compared with, respectively, 59 percent and 40 percent of the men.[33]

TABLE 3-3

Gender Differences in Support for Affirmative Action Programs to Help Women Get Better Jobs and a Better Education, by Age Group (percent)

Age Group	Men		Women	
	Favor	Oppose	Favor	Oppose
18–29	55	22	73	9
30–44	48	35	63	24
45–64	59	31	75	9
65+	40	39	71	16

Source: Los Angeles Times survey, March 15–19, 1995. Reported in *Public Perspective* 6, no. 4 (June/July 1995): 39.

Note: The question was: "Are you in favor of affirmative action programs designed to help women get better jobs and education, or are you opposed to them, or haven't you heard enough to say?"

However, support for affirmative action varies with the wording of the survey question, as is evident from a comparison of the pattern of responses to the question asking whether respondents support "affirmative action programs designed to help women get better jobs and education" (Table 3-3) to the response pattern when the question refers to giving preference in hiring or promotion "where there has been job discrimination against women in the past" (Tables 3-4 and 3-5). Support also varies by level of education; those with some college or a college degree are generally less supportive, although within each educational grouping women are more supportive than men of giving preferences to women in hiring, to overcome the results of past discrimination against women (see Table 3-5). Women are also more likely to believe that affirmative action programs are still necessary to protect women from discrimination,[34] and that affirmative action programs designed to help women get better jobs and a better education do not go too far and are not adequate.[35]

Is there a white male backlash against affirmative action programs for women? A 1995 Louis Harris survey suggests that if one exists, it is not based on personal experiences in the workplace. When men were asked, "Do you feel that your employer has been doing too much, too little, or about the right amount to hire and promote women employees?" only 9 percent said "too much" and 11 percent said "too little"; 69 percent responded that their employer was "doing about the right amount."[36]

One issue that concerns values relating to equality is the appropriate role for women serving in the military. Men and women differ in their attitudes

TABLE 3-4

Gender Differences in Support for Affirmative Action Programs in Hiring or Promotion of Women, by Age Group (percent)

Age Group	Men		Women	
	Favor	Oppose	Favor	Oppose
18–29	37	63	54	42
30–44	37	58	52	39
45–64	35	61	51	41
65+	34	54	41	43

Source: CBS/New York Times survey, April 1–4, 1995. Reported in Public Perspective 6, no. 4 (June/July 1995): 39.

Note: The question was: "Where there has been job discrimination against women in the past, preference in hiring or promotion should be given" to women?

on this issue. In a 1993 survey, almost four-fifths of the women and slightly more than half the men said they approved of allowing women to assume combat roles.[37]

SEXUAL HARASSMENT. The problem of sexual harassment of women is not new; however, its importance as a political issue escalated with the Supreme Court nomination of Clarence Thomas and the allegations presented at his confirmation hearings before the Senate Judiciary Committee in October 1991. Attorney Anita Hill, a former employee of the Equal Employment Opportunity Commission when it was chaired by Clarence Thomas, alleged that he had displayed a persistent pattern of sexual harassment toward her. Feminists claimed that the all-male Judiciary Committee "did not get it," igniting a firestorm of controversy and again focusing national attention on the problem of sexual harassment.[38] In 1992 the American National Election Study survey found that men and women differed significantly in their perception that sexual harassment was a serious workplace problem (38 percent of the women compared with 25 percent of the men). Women (41 percent) were more likely than men (31 percent) to report that they or someone they knew had experienced sexual harassment at work. A majority of the men and almost two-thirds of the women thought too little was being done to protect women from sexual harassment. When asked, "If a woman says she has been sexually harassed at work and the man denies it, would you be more inclined to believe the woman or the man?" 44 percent of the men and 62 percent of the women

TABLE 3-5

Gender Differences in Support for Affirmative Action Programs in Hiring or Promotion of Women, by Level of Educational Attainment (percent)

Educational Attainment Level	Men		Women	
	Favor	Oppose	Favor	Oppose
High school or less	42	53	55	35
Some college	23	74	48	41
College graduate	31	66	36	58

Source: CBS/*New York Times* survey, April 1–4, 1995. Reported in *Public Perspective* 6, no. 4 (June/July 1995): 39.

Note: The question was: "Where there has been job discrimination against women in the past, preference in hiring or promotion should be given" to women?

responded that they would be more likely to believe the woman. But 47 percent of the men and 34 percent of the women indicated it would depend on the circumstances related to the allegation.[39]

TRUSTWORTHINESS AND EFFECTIVENESS OF THE FEDERAL GOVERNMENT. To what extent do men and women differ in the trust they place in the federal government and in their sense of its political effectiveness? Table 3-6 shows their responses to four survey questions, three of which were developed as measures of trust:

1. How much of the time do you think you can trust the government in Washington to do what is right—just about always, most of the time or only some of the time?
2. Would you say the government is pretty much run by a few big interests looking out for themselves or that it is run for the benefit of all the people?
3. Do you think the people in the government waste a lot of the money we pay in taxes, waste some of it, or don't waste very much of it?

Between 1964 and 1994, trust in the government in Washington declined dramatically among both men and women, especially as measured by responses to the first two questions. However, only infrequently have there been significant gender differences in the responses to these questions.[40] In several years (1968, 1972, 1984, and 1992), women were substantially less likely than men to believe that the federal government wastes a lot of tax money. A possible explanation for this is that in general, women are more supportive of several types of domestic policy programs. Despite the few significant differences between men and women revealed by these responses, one pattern is clear: trust in the federal government declined substantially from 1972 to 1992.

Another attitude indicative of what people think about government is their sense of its political efficacy, or personal political effectiveness. This attitude has two components: (1) the feeling that people like oneself can be effective in politics (internal efficacy); (2) the belief that the federal government is responsive to the views of people like oneself (external efficacy). Table 3-6 concerns one indicator of *external* political efficacy, response to the statement that "I don't think public officials care much what people like me think." The proportion of survey respondents who say they believe that public officials don't care much "what people like me think" has increased substantially since 1964, but no significant differences exist between men and women in their responses to this statement.

KNOWLEDGE AS BASIS OF INFORMED OPINION. Men and women differ in their level of political knowledge; men are more knowledgeable about both governmental processes and current events. Several explanations for this difference can be suggested. Women are less likely to work outside the home or to have jobs that stimulate political interest and a feeling of political efficacy. In addition, in most families women have primary responsibility for child care, housework (cooking, cleaning, and doing the laundry), and elder care. They therefore have less time to acquire political information by reading newspapers and newsmagazines, watching television news, and engaging in political discussions.

Older women (age 65 and older) are also likely to have lower levels of educational attainment than older men. As recently as 1993, women were less likely than men to have completed four or more years of college.[41] Thus, we would expect women as a group to have less knowledge about the federal government's structure and processes. Women are as knowledgeable as men about local government and politics, however. When knowledge levels of women are compared to those of men with similar occupational status and levels of income and education, women are found to be less knowledgeable about national government and politics. One explanation is that many women were raised in families in which the socially accepted gender role expectations for women did not include being interested in politics and being politically active.[42]

TABLE 3-6
Gender Differences in Attitudes toward the Federal Government, 1964–1994 (percent)

Year	Trust the Government Most of the Time or Just about Always		Government Is Run by a Few Big Interests		Government Wastes a Lot of Money		Public Officials Do Not Care Much What People Like Me Think	
	Men	Women	Men	Women	Men	Women	Men	Women
1964	80	76	32	30	51	46	37	37
1968	62	63	49	39	66	56	42	45
1972	55	54	59	58	71	64	49	51
1976	36	34	74	73	77	76	52	55
1980	26	26	78	76	82	79	54	55
1984	43	46	60	57	72	62	42	43
1988	43	40	66	68	66	62	52	51
1992	28	30	79	78	72	65	53	52
1994	21	22	80	80	72	70	66	66

Source: Calculated from data in the 1952–1992 American National Election Studies Cumulative File and the 1994 American National Election Study.

Measures of Political Orientation

PARTY IDENTIFICATION. The schema is a device developed by cognitive psychologists to explain how individuals differentially structure their patterns of thought about political objects. More specifically, a schema is "a cognitive structure that represents organized knowledge about a given concept or type of stimulus. A schema contains both the attributes of the concept and the relationships among the attributes."[43] Schema theory assumes that information is stored in abstract form. Schemata are theories about how individuals perceive, remember, and reason about reality. Thus individuals act as cognitive misers, in that they use schemata to construct individualistic versions of reality. Schemata permit the interpretation of specific instances in terms of generalizations based on other, existing schemata.

Individuals differ in the nature and structure of the schemas used to assess and process cognitive stimuli. For example, research suggests that evangelical Christian women have a different cognitive structure than nonevangelical women. Evangelical women are less likely to believe that women should have an equal role with men and that the federal government should help improve the socioeconomic status of women; they are also less likely to endorse abortion on demand.[44]

One attribute within a cognitive schema that can have a significant impact on patterns of political attitudes and on some types of political behavior is party identification. In the United States, an individual's sense of identity with a political party affects the perceived qualities of candidates for elective office, evaluation of the job performance of elected officials, and approval (or disapproval) of policies advocated by candidates, elected officials, and political party leaders. Gender differences in party identification began to develop in the early 1970s, and that is still the prevailing pattern.[45] Since 1972, more women than men have reported an affiliation with the Democratic Party or have usually voted for candidates of the Democratic Party (see Figure 3-1). The proportion of both men and women who declare themselves to be independent has increased since the 1970s. Gender differences in party identification can be explained in part by the movement of some men to the Republican Party beginning in the 1960s.[46]

In the 1990s, gender differences in party identification have been greatest among younger voters (age 18 to 35); men are more likely to be Republicans and women are more likely to be Democrats. Women college

FIGURE 3-1
Gender Differences in Party Identification, 1952–1992

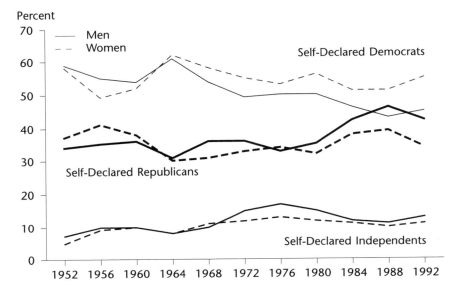

Source: 1952–1992 American National Election Studies Cumulative File, variable 301.

graduates in that age group are more likely to be Republicans than are women with lower levels of educational attainment, but they are less likely to be Republicans than college-educated men in the same age group.[47]

CANDIDATE PREFERENCE. One dimension of gender differences in political orientation is the evaluation of candidates for elective office. Gender differences in patterns of voting for president have been evident for several decades. Prior to 1964, women were more likely than men to vote for Republican presidential candidates. Beginning with the 1964 presidential election, however, women were more likely than men to vote for Democratic presidential candidates.

In the 1990s, men and women have differed significantly in their evaluation of independent presidential candidate Ross Perot.[48] During the 1992 presidential election, women were significantly less likely than men to support Perot. Some survey data on candidate support indicate that men were almost equally divided between Bush and Clinton. Women were significantly more likely to choose Democratic candidate Bill Clinton rather than Republican candidate George Bush. The higher their level of educational attainment and income level, the more supportive women were of Clinton.[49] Women's support for Clinton also varied with marital status; married women were significantly less likely to vote for him than were women who had never married or who were divorced or separated. This "marriage gap" has also occurred in some prior presidential elections; married women were more likely to support the Republican candidate. However, in the 1992 election, married men were much less likely than unmarried men to support Clinton. These patterns of candidate support were also evident in the 1996 election (see Chapter 7).

In 1993, gender differences in evaluations of Perot continued to exist. Women were significantly less likely to support him; the differences were particularly striking among younger voters. Republican men in all age groups were almost twice as likely as Republican women to support the former presidential candidate.[50]

To what extent are women willing to support women candidates for elective office? Analyses of voting patterns suggest that under certain conditions, women are more likely than men to vote for women candidates. In 35 statewide contests for the U.S. Senate or for a state governor from 1980 to 1990, the gender difference in voting patterns was 10 percent or greater. In five other contests, a plurality of women voted for the woman candidate and a plurality of men voted for the man. In all of these statewide races, Democratic women candidates usually attracted women's votes (16 out of 19 contests); Republican women candidates attracted women's votes in only 3 out of 16 contests. The ability of Democratic women candidates to increase voter turnout and attract votes increased during the 1980s. During this period women were less supportive of Republican candidates than were men, regardless of the Republican candidate's gender. This gender gap was evident in presidential elections as well as in races for the U.S. Senate and in gubernatorial contests.[51]

NOTES

1. Sue Tolleson-Rinehart, *Gender Consciousness and Politics* (New York: Routledge, 1992), 14.

2. See Patricia Gurin, "Women's Gender Consciousness," *Public Opinion Quarterly* 49 (1985), 143–163; Patricia Gurin, Arthur H. Miller, and Gerald Gurin, "Stratum Identification and Consciousness," *Social Psychology Quarterly* 43 (1980): 30–47; and Arthur H. Miller, Patricia Gurin, Gerald Gurin, and Oksana

Malanchuk, "Group Consciousness and Political Participation," *American Journal of Political Science* 25 (1981): 494–511. Pamela Johnson Conover and Virginia Sapiro, in "Gender, Feminist Consciousness, and War," *American Journal of Political Science* 37 (November 1993), argue that "the cognitive core of feminist consciousness is an awareness of and sensitivity to the unequal and gendered nature of society (empirical sexual equality), and a commitment to ending the inequalities (normative sexual equality)" (1084). Three aspects of feminist consciousness are measured: "a commitment to normative sexual equality, a feminist identity, and a sense of emotional bond with women" (1086).

3. See Herbert Hyman, *Political Socialization* (New York: Free Press, 1959); David Easton and Jack Dennis, *Children in the Political System* (New York: McGraw-Hill, 1969); Fred I. Greenstein, *Children and Politics* (New Haven: Yale University Press, 1965); and Robert E. Hess and Judith V. Torney, *The Development of Political Attitudes in Children* (Chicago: Aldine, 1967).

4. Diana Owen and Jack Dennis, "Gender Differences in the Politicization of American Children," *Women and Politics* 8 (no. 2) (1988): 23–43.

5. Research conducted by Owen and Dennis in 1985 (ibid., Table 1) indicated that in 8 of 15 politicization measures, no significant differences existed between young males and young females; in 7 of 15 politicization measures, no significant differences existed between older males and older females.

6. Sandra Bowman Damico, Alfonso J. Damico, and M. Margaret Conway, "Students Who Become Citizens: Schools and Democracy," paper prepared for the Youth 2000 Conference, University of Teesside, Middlesbrough, England, July 19–22, 1995.

7. Roberta S. Sigel and John V. Reynolds, "Generational Differences and the Women's Movement," *Political Science Quarterly* 94 (1979–1980): 635–648.

8. Pamela Johnston Conover suggests that a feminist identity and consciousness, once developed, leads to a redefinition of the values created by earlier socialization and such factors as educational attainment, employment history, and family experiences. These changed values affect both the salience of issues and issue preferences. See Conover, "Feminists and the Gender Gap," *Journal of Politics* 50 (November 1988): 984–1010.

9. See C. Richard Hofstetter and William A. Schultze, "Some Observations about Participation and Attitudes among Single Parent Women: Inferences Concerning Political Translation," *Women and Politics* 9 (1989): 83–105; M. Kent Jennings, "Gender Roles and Inequalities in Political Participation," *Western Political Quarterly* 37 (1983): 364–385; Ronald B. Rapoport, "The Sex Gap in Political Persuading," *American Journal of Political Science* 25 (1981): 32–48; Virginia Sapiro, *The Political Integration of Women* (Urbana: University of Illinois Press, 1983); and Clyde Wilcox, "Black Women and Feminism," *Women and Politics* 10 (1980): 65–84.

10. It is adherence to evangelical doctrine, not the particular religious denom-

ination, that is significant in its impact. Only with regard to views on abortion does evangelical denomination attain statistical significance. See Clyde Wilcox and Elizabeth Adell Cook, "Evangelical Women and Feminism: Some Additional Evidence," *Women and Politics* 9 (1989): 27–49.

11. Clyde Wilcox, "Feminism and Anti-Feminism among White Evangelical Women," *Western Political Quarterly* 42 (1989): 147–160.

12. Wilcox and Cook, "Evangelical Women and Feminism," 35.

13. 1992 American National Election Study, variable 3701.

14. Ibid., variables 3701, 3716, and 3707.

15. Ibid., variable 3603.

16. Ibid., variables 3726, 3728, 3729–3731, and 3813–3819 pertain to preferences on government spending for various policies.

17. "Women and the Use of Force," in The American Enterprise, *Public Perspective* 5, no. 5 (July/August 1994): 96.

18. Ibid. See Robert Shapiro and Harpreet Mahajan, "Gender Differences in Policy Preferences: A Summary of Trends from the 1960s to the 1980s," *Public Opinion Quarterly* 50 (1986): 42–61. Shapiro and Mahajan found moderately large differences in preferences concerning the use of force. The salience of this issue for women appears to have increased over time. See also Tom Smith, "The Polls: Gender and Attitudes toward Violence," *Public Opinion Quarterly* 48 (1984): 384–396.

19. James A. Davis and Tom W. Smith, *General Social Surveys, 1972–1994: Cumulative File* (Chicago: National Opinion Research Center). The terms "traumatic abortion" and "elective abortion" were first used in Elizabeth Adell Cook, Ted G. Jelen, and Clyde Wilcox, *Between Two Absolutes: Public Opinion and the Politics of Abortion* (Boulder, Colo.: Westview Press, 1992), 33–38, 48.

20. Cook, Jelen, and Wilcox, *Between Two Absolutes,* 44; National Opinion Research Center, General Social Survey, 1994.

21. 1992 American National Election Study, variables 3732 and 3735–3740.

22. Cook, Jelen, and Wilcox, *Between Two Absolutes*, 48–49.

23. M. Margaret Conway, David W. Ahern, and Gertrude A. Steuernagel, *Women and Public Policy: A Revolution in Progress* (Washington, D.C.: CQ Press, 1995), 64–67.

24. Judith A. Baer, *Women in American Law* (New York: Holmes and Meier, 1991), 77–78.

25. Conway, Ahern, and Steuernagel, *Women and Public Policy,* 69; Dorothy McBride Stetson, *Women's Rights in the U.S.A.* (Pacific Grove, Calif.: Brooks/Cole, 1991), 168–173.

26. Baer, *Women in American Law,* chap. 3; Susan Gleck Mezey, *In Pursuit of Equality: Women, Public Policy, and the Federal Courts* (New York: St. Martin's Press, 1992), chap. 4.

27. NBC/*Wall Street Journal* survey, March 4–7, 1995; reported in *Public*

Perspective 6, no. 4 (June/July 1995): 33.

28. CBS/*New York Times* survey, April 1–4, 1995; reported in ibid.

29. Princeton Survey Research Associates survey, February 1–3, 1995, reported in ibid.

30. Greenberg-Lake, The Analysis Group survey, May 26–June 8, 1992, reported in ibid., 34.

31. Roper Center survey, August 22–29, 1994, reported in ibid.

32. Gallup poll, March 17–19, 1995, reported in ibid.

33. Roper Center survey, August 22–29, 1994, reported in ibid., 39.

34. CBS/*New York Times* survey, April 1–4, 1995, reported in ibid.

35. *Los Angeles Times* survey, March 15–19, 1995, ibid., 41.

36. Humphrey Taylor, "The White Male Backlash, If It Exists, Is Not Based on Personal Experiences in the Workplace," Harris poll press release, Harris poll no. 44, July 17, 1995. Survey was conducted June 8–11, 1995.

37. *Los Angeles Times* survey, February 11–16, 1993, reported in The American Enterprise, *Public Perspective* 4, no. 5 (July/August 1993): 102.

38. According to the Sexual Harassment Guidelines issued by the Equal Employment Opportunity Commission, sexual harassment is a form of sexual discrimination. In the *Code of Federal Regulations,* 29 C.F.R. chap. 14, sec. 1604.11 (1996), sexual harassment is defined as follows:

> Unwelcome sexual advances, requests for sexual favors, and other verbal or physical conduct of a sexual nature constitute sexual harassment when (1) submission to such conduct is made either explicitly or implicitly a term or condition of an individual's employment, (2) submission to or rejection of such conduct by an individual is used as the basis for employment or academic decisions affecting such individual, or (3) such conduct has the purpose or effect of unreasonably interfering with an individual's work performance or creating an intimidating, hostile, or offensive working environment.

39. 1992 American National Election Study, variables 3741–3744.

40. Ibid., variables 6103 and 6120–6122. In 1976, the first presidential election year after Richard Nixon resigned as president, a significantly smaller proportion of women (compared with earlier years) trusted the federal government most of the time or just about always. Nixon was facing the threat of impeachment charges brought by the House of Representatives and conviction by the Senate as a consequence of illegal activities by members of his campaign staff during the 1972 campaign and his participation in the cover-up of those activities. In 1968, a significantly smaller proportion of women (compared with 1972 and subsequent years) believed the government to be run by a few big interests.

41. U.S. Department of Commerce, Economics and Statistics Administration, Bureau of the Census, *Statistical Abstract of the United States, 1994* (Washington, D.C.: 1994), Table 233, 157.

42. Michael X. Delli Carpini and Scott Keeter, "The Gender Gap in Political Knowledge," *Public Perspective* 3, no. 5 (July/August 1992): 23–26.

43. Susan T. Fiske and Shelley E. Taylor, *Social Cognition* (Reading, Mass.: Addison-Wesley, 1984), 140; see also 141–142. For a discussion of different types of schema, see 148–170, especially Table 6.1.

44. Wilcox and Cook, "Evangelical Women and Feminism," 27–49.

45. Gallup Omnibus survey and CNN/*USA Today* survey, October 1991–May 1992, reported in *Public Perspective* 3, no. 5 (July/August 1992): 27–28.

46. Mary E. Bendyna and Celinda C. Lake, "Gender and Voting in the 1992 Presidential Election," in Elizabeth Adell Cook, Sue Thomas, and Clyde Wilcox, *The Year of the Woman* (Boulder, Colo.: Westview Press, 1994), 238–239.

47. *Public Perspective* 7, no. 5 (August/September 1996): 16.

48. Paul R. Abramson, John H. Aldrich, and David W. Rohde, *Change and Continuity in the 1992 Elections,* rev. ed. (Washington, D.C.: CQ Press, 1995), 136.

49. Ibid.

50. Gallup polls, March, April, and June 1993, reported in The American Enterprise, *Public Perspective* 4, no. 5 (July/August 1993): 98.

51. Tom Smith and Lance A. Selfa, "When Do Women Vote for Women?" *Public Perspective* 3, no. 6 (September/October 1992): 30–31.

SUGGESTIONS FOR FURTHER READING

Dentzer, Susan. "Coming in '96: Shoot-out at the Gender Gap?" *Working Woman,* 20, no. 11 (November 1995): 9.

Fitzpatrick, Kellyanne. "Gender Gap Politics: The Republican Warning." *Campaigns and Elections* 16, no. 10 (October 1995): 25–26.

Hayes, Bernadette, and Clive S. Bean. "Political Attitudes and Partisanship among Australian Couples: Do Wives Matter?" *Women and Politics* 14, no. 1 (1994): 53–81.

Herrick, Rebekah. "Is There a Gender Gap in the Value of Campaign Resources?" *American Politics Quarterly* 24, no. 1 (January 1996): 68–80.

Lake, Celinda. "Gender Gap Politics: The Democratic Puzzle." *Campaigns and Elections* 16, no. 10 (October 1995): 23–24.

Pierce, Patrick. "Gender Role and Political Culture: The Electoral Connection." *Women and Politics* 9, no. 1 (1989): 21–46.

Somma, Mark. "The Gender Gap and Attitudes towards Economic Development among Midwestern Adults." *Women and Politics* 12, no. 2 (1992): 41–57.

CHAPTER 4

Differences among Women: Does Group Identification Explain Political Orientation?

PATTERNS OF GROUP CONSCIOUSNESS

Mary and Stacy grew up in the same city and attended the same high school and college. Both now work for large banks in the same city. Their social and political views, however, are quite different.

Stacy supports an equal role for men and women in business, government, and industry, whereas Mary believes that women should always be subordinate to men and should never have an equal role in decision making. Stacy believes the women's movement has made a major, positive contribution to improving conditions for women; Mary opposes the women's movement. These two women represent different identifications. Stacy is an example of a feminist; Mary is an example of a nonfeminist.

The preceding analysis is based on what sociologists label a categoric group. The assignment of individuals to a particular categoric group is based on demographic characteristics such as sex, age, income level, and the region in which they live. Thus someone who is 80 years old and lives in Georgia is "an elderly Southerner." In the preceding analysis, individuals are assigned to one of two groups, according to their sex.

The attitudes, beliefs, and behavior of individuals can also be analyzed on the basis of the extent of their psychological identification with a particular group—their group consciousness. To what extent do women identify with women as a group? Do women's political orientations and political activity vary with their level of group consciousness? The hypothesis examined here is that women who identify with other women have similar perceptions of the problems facing women and are more likely to engage in political and social actions that may directly or indirectly alleviate those common problems. This shared identity is called gender consciousness. Women may have gender consciousness yet have different views of the problems that women encounter and the best solutions for those problems, however. For example, during the last decades of the twentieth century, the leaders of politically conservative women's groups such as the National Organization for Women and the Women's Equity Action League, which have as their goals equality of opportunity for women in society, business, and politics, have had very different views and policy preferences on many issues.

The components of group consciousness include social group identification and the sharing of perceptions of problems and interests with other group members. Other components of group consciousness include being discontented with the group's power compared with that of other social groups, viewing perceived disparities as illegitimate, and having a collective orientation toward solving shared problems.[1] A label given to this kind of group consciousness among women is "feminist consciousness."

Several measures of the extent to which women share a feminist group consciousness have been created and used in research on women's group identification patterns and their political effects. One measure uses the survey item measuring feeling close to women as a group combined with a measure of levels of support for an equal role for women.[2] Another uses an individual's relative evaluations of labels commonly applied to the modern women's movement (the women's liberation movement, the women's movement, or feminists) together with a measure of levels of support for an equal role for women.[3]

Among components of women's group consciousness are discontent with women's power relative to that of other groups in society and viewing the perceived disparities as illegitimate. An indicator of these components of group consciousness is a survey item that has been included in the American National Election Studies since 1972:

> Recently there has been a lot of talk about women's rights. Some people
> feel that women should have an equal role with men in running business,

industry, and government. Others feel that women's place is in the home. Where would you place yourself on this scale, or haven't you thought much about this?[4]

Support for an equal role for women is generally agreed to be a component of feminist consciousness. The opposite view of the appropriate role for women is that "women's place is in the home." This traditional view emphasizes the domestic roles of wife and mother in a patriarchal society, in which women are subordinate to men. It was predominant in American society until the second half of the twentieth century, when the perspective changed dramatically.

Table 4-1 shows the response patterns of women and men to the preceding question in surveys conducted in election years 1972 through 1994. In 1992, a higher percentage of women (56 percent) than men (50 percent) placed themselves at the strongest level of support for an equal role for women; in 1994, these proportions declined to 42 percent of the men and 47 percent of the women. However, if the proportions selecting the three scores supporting an equal role for women (1, 2, and 3) are added together, in both 1992 and 1994 approximately equal proportions of men and women (almost 75 percent) supported an equal role for women.

Studies using data from a panel study of individuals surveyed in 1973 and again in 1982 found a similar trend toward more support for an equal role for women.[5] Another study has found that for all individuals except those with the most limited cognitive ability, attitudes with regard to equal roles are associated with patterns of political attitudes.[6]

The extent to which women feel close to other women is one measure of social group identification, a key component of group consciousness. The survey of the American electorate conducted in national election years by researchers at the University of Michigan (the American National Election Study) includes an item that asks those interviewed to indicate which groups they feel close to; one of the groups listed is women. The survey respondents are then asked to indicate which group they feel closest to. Since 1972, the proportion of women who report feeling close to women as a group has ranged from 35 percent to 49 percent, and the proportion of women reporting they feel closest to women has ranged from 8.4 percent to 10.6 percent.[7]

Another way to measure the extent to which women identify with women as a group is to ask survey respondents to indicate their feelings toward a variety of groups by rating each group on a "feeling thermome-

TABLE 4-1

Continuum Ranking of Gender Differences in Support for Equal Role for Women, 1972–1994 (percent)

Ranking[a]	1972 Men	1972 Women	1976 Men	1976 Women	1980 Men	1980 Women	1984 Men	1984 Women	1988 Men	1988 Women	1992 Men	1992 Women	1994 Men	1994 Women
1 (Equal role for women)	33	33	34	33	35	35	36	36	40	46	50	56	42	47
2	11	8	14	8	18	10	16	11	19	13	17	12	20	14
3	8	6	11	10	9	8	11	10	10	10	8	6	8	8
4	18	22	18	21	15	19	23	24	17	16	14	14	15	17
5	7	6	9	8	9	6	8	8	6	4	5	4	5	7
6	5	4	5	5	8	6	3	4	4	4	3	2	4	3
7 (Women's place is in the home)	18	21	9	14	6	7	4	7	5	7	3	4	3	4

Source: Calculated from data in the 1952–1992 American National Election Studies Cumulative File and the 1994 American National Election Study.

[a] 1 = strongest level of support for an equal role for women; 7 = strongest level of support for "women's place is in the home."

ter," whose readings range from 100 (the most positive) to zero (the most negative). A reading of 50 is neutral, readings of 51 and above are positive, and those of 49 and below are negative. From 1972 to 1984, women were asked to rate the "women's liberation movement," as the modern women's movement was called in the 1960s and 1970s; in 1988 and 1992, they were asked to rate "feminists";[8] in 1992 they were asked to rate the "women's movement."[9] Group identification among women from 1972 to 1992, as measured by their ratings of three women's groups on the feeling thermometer, is indicated by the absolute mean scores in the first row of Table 4-2. Of course, it would be preferable to have evaluations of the same group (either the women's liberation movement, feminists, or the women's movement) over time. However, beginning in 1988, either "feminists" or the "women's movement" (rather than the "women's liberation movement") was used in these surveys. In 1992, both the "women's movement" and "feminists" were used. Thus both sets of responses can be used to construct feminist consciousness scales, and the results obtained by using a different group in the surveys can then be compared.[10] These measures of feminist consciousness enable us to evaluate the extent of women's social group identification and the impact of feminist consciousness on patterns of political behavior and political attitudes.[11]

To evaluate the extent of women's feminist consciousness, we can analyze the patterns that are evident when responses to questions on group closeness are combined with responses to questions pertaining to the equal role for women versus women's place is in the home. Sue Tolleson-Rinehart established three categories of women, based on their responses to the group closeness questions: not close to other women, close, and closest.[12] The proportion reporting that they felt close to women ranged from 34 percent in 1972 to 62 percent in 1984. The proportion declined to 43 percent in 1988, and in 1992 it was 36 percent. The proportion that reported feeling closest to women, of all the groups considered, ranged from 10.6 percent in 1976 to 6.7 percent in 1984.[13] In the years that this question was asked, the number of groups included ranged from 15 to 19.

The proportion of women identifying with and feeling close to other women varies with the race, occupation, and educational attainment level of those being interviewed. Women of color are more likely to report feeling close to women than are white women. Those who are middle class or higher in their subjective social class placement and those with higher levels of family and individual incomes are more likely to identify with other women; housewives are less likely to do so. Women with higher levels of

TABLE 4-2
Feminist Consciousness among Women, 1972–1992

| | Women's Liberation Movement | | | | | Feminists | | Women's Movement |
	1972	1976	1980	1984	1988	1992a	1992b
Absolute mean score (feeling thermometer)	45	53	62	63	62	61	61
Adjusted mean score (feeling thermometer)	-.23	.91	.90	.94	.87	.88	1.01
Average equal role score	3.5	3.3	2.9	3.0	2.6	2.2	2.2
Distribution of feminist consciousness scores							
None	63	53	43	48	37	29	29
Potential	27	28	35	35	48	53	40
Feminist	10	19	22	17	14	18	30

Source: Calculated from data in the 1952–1990 American National Election Studies Cumulative File and the 1992 American National Election Study.

Note: Based on responses to equal roles question and feeling thermometer scores for the women's liberation movement (1972 to 1984), feminists (1988 and 1992a), and the women's movement (1992b).

education are more likely to report identifying with other women and feeling close to women as a group.[14]

Although feeling close to other women is a component of gender consciousness, that alone does not indicate the existence of feminist consciousness. As was pointed out earlier, women may feel close to other women and yet have very different views about appropriate roles for women in society. Those who believe that women should not have an equal role have a "privatized" perspective on the preferred role for women.[15] Women may be gender conscious but not feminist. It is the interaction of different dimensions of attitudes that determines whether one is feminist.

In examining the patterns of women's closeness to other women and their beliefs about an equal role for women, Tolleson-Rinehart established six categories of feminist orientation: individualist and privatized; identify with women and privatized; individualist and ambivalent; identify with women and ambivalent; individualist and egalitarian; and identify with women and egalitarian. The proportion of women survey respondents who reported not feeling close to other women and who viewed women's appropriate role as being "in the home" decreased from 22.8 percent in 1972 to 7.9 percent in 1988; the proportion who reported not feeling close to other women but who were supportive of an equal role for women increased from 31.1 percent in 1972 to 43.4 percent in 1988. As might be expected, among those who reported feeling close to other women and those who said they felt closest to women, in this period there was a decline in the proportion believing that women's place is in the home and an increase in the proportion supporting an equal role for women.[16] Tolleson-Rinehart argues that changes in women's gender consciousness (traditional, ambivalent, or feminist) influence their political beliefs and attitudes, political activity, and support for policy measures. Her research supports that argument.[17]

Women's gender consciousness derives from their beliefs about appropriate roles for women. Those who have feminist consciousness are aware of women's traditionally subordinate roles in society and the discrimination against women in a variety of social roles. Resentment of that pattern of discrimination may give rise to a collective orientation. However, other outcomes are also possible. Some women admit that women in general have suffered as a result of systematic discrimination but consider themselves to be exceptions. Roberta Sigel calls this the "not me" coping strategy. Another coping strategy is to "work harder" and excel on one's own. Women who adopt these approaches do not develop a collective orientation.[18]

An alternative method for evaluating feminist consciousness is to use the feeling thermometer ratings of the labels for the modern women's movement in combination with the scores indicating level of support for an equal role for women. Proponents of this method, which was developed by Elizabeth Adell Cook, point out that individuals differ in how positively they rate all groups, whereas an increase in the proportion of women who report they feel close to other women has been evident since the early 1970s. In addition, the closeness measure does not correlate highly with other components of group consciousness (discontent, system blame, and collective orientation) or with the feeling thermometer measure for the women's liberation movement.[19]

We can explore the extent to which women differ in their levels of political participation by using this alternative measure of feminist consciousness. The feeling thermometer score must be adjusted for individuals' tendencies to vary in the ratings they give to groups. To do so, a mean feeling thermometer score is created by adding together the ratings given to nine groups (big business, labor unions, whites, blacks, liberals, conservatives, the military, the poor, and civil rights leaders) in all years except 1992. (In 1992 the civil rights leaders measure was not included in the survey.) This score is then divided by the number of groups rated. Thus the following equation is used to calculate this component of the feminist consciousness score:

Mean feeling thermometer score = sum of ratings of each of the groups divided by the number of groups (8 in 1992; 9 in other years)

Some individuals tend to give high (or low) ratings to all groups. Therefore, the feeling thermometer rating given by each individual to the women's group label (the women's liberation movement, feminists, or the women's movement) must be adjusted in accordance with that individual's rating patterns. The following formula is used:

$$\frac{\text{Individual's rating of the women's group label} - \text{individual's mean rating of all groups}}{\text{Individual's mean rating of all groups}}$$

The result is an index score. If an individual's rating of the women's group label is equal to the individual's mean rating of all nine (or eight) groups, her relative rating of the women's group label is higher and the result will be a positive score; if it is lower, the result will be a negative score. Using the same criteria used by Cook, we will consider an individual rating that is 10 percent or more below the individual's mean rating of all groups a negative evaluation.[20]

This index score, or relative feeling thermometer rating, is combined with the individual's score on the equal role question to create a feminist consciousness measure. The equal role question requires survey respondents to place themselves on a seven-point scale, with 1 indicating support for an equal role for women and 7 indicating agreement with the statement that "women's place is in the home." Women who place themselves at 4 (neutral) or at 5, 6, or 7 (believe that women's place is in the home) are classified as lacking feminist consciousness. Women who place themselves at one or 2 (strongly favor an equal role for women) and whose rating of the women's group label is at least 10 percent above their mean rating of other groups are classified as feminists. Those who favor an equal role for women but whose rating of the women's group is less than 10 percent of their mean rating of other groups are classified as potential feminists.

The pattern of feminist consciousness has clearly changed over time. The distribution of feminist consciousness scores and the women's scores on the feeling thermometer in presidential election years 1972 to 1992 are shown in Table 4-2. Use of the measure based on ratings of the women's liberation movement, from 1972 to 1984, reveals a significant decline in the proportion of women who lack feminist consciousness: from 63 percent in 1972 to 48 percent in 1984. There was a corresponding increase in the proportion of women with a potential for feminist consciousness: from 27 percent in 1972 to 35 percent in 1984.[21] If we use the measure based on ratings of feminists from 1988 to 1992, we note a similar trend: the proportion of nonfeminists declined and the proportions of potential feminists and feminists increased.

Using the measure of feminist support based in part on evaluations of the women's movement in 1992, we find that 29 percent of the women surveyed were nonfeminists, 40 percent were potential feminists, and 30 percent were feminists. What sociodemographic characteristics distinguish feminists from potential feminists and these two groups from nonfeminists?

Analysis of the data reveals the existence of significant generational differences concerning this measure of feminist support in 1992; support for feminism is inversely related to age. The women of generation X are strongest in their support for feminism; almost 50 percent can be categorized as feminists. In contrast, 40 percent of the younger baby boomer women and less than one-third of those aged 47 and older are feminists.[22]

Feminist support varies with educational attainment level. Those with higher levels of education are more likely to be feminists; 45 percent of those with some college study or a bachelor's degree and 61 percent of those with advanced degrees can be categorized as feminists. In contrast, less than 20 percent of those who did not graduate from high school and less than 30 percent of high school graduates are feminists. Feminist support among married women in the sample varies with the spouse's educational attainment level; 45 percent of those whose husbands attended college are feminists compared with less than 20 percent of those whose husbands did not graduate from high school and less than 30 percent of those whose husbands were high school graduates.

Support for feminism varies with employment status. In 1992, 41 percent of the employed women, 46 percent of the unemployed women seeking work, 54 percent of the full-time students, and 67 percent of the students who were also working less than 20 hours per week can be classified as feminists. In comparison, only 24 percent of homemakers are classified as feminists.

The higher the occupational status of employed women, the more likely they are to be categorized as feminists: 50 percent of those holding executive and administrative positions and 54 percent of those in professional positions are feminists, whereas less than one-third of the women having blue-collar jobs are in that category.

RELATION OF FEMINIST ORIENTATION TO POLITICAL ATTITUDES AND POLICY PREFERENCES

Do women's political attitudes and patterns of political participation vary with their degree of support for feminism? If their political attitudes do vary, is the pattern consistent across attitudinal categories, or do attitudes vary with the issue?[23]

Support for Federal Government Programs

To examine the extent to which political attitudes and policy preferences vary with women's feminist support categories, we can use a number of the policy preference questions that were included in the 1992 American National Election Study. Citizens of voting age were asked if they would prefer to have the federal government spend more money, less money, or the same amount of money on a particular program. Significant differences are evident among women (categorized as feminists, potential feminists, and nonfeminists) in their support for federal spending for child care, aid to the unemployed, environmental programs, welfare programs, the homeless problem, public schools, and urban assistance.[24] Feminists were more supportive than potential feminists or nonfeminists of increased federal funding for all of these programs. Feminists did not differ significantly from other categories in support for funding for crime prevention, aid to the poor, and aid to college students.[25] On the question of increased federal spending, if necessary, to maintain the United States as the world's preeminent military power, nonfeminists were more supportive than potential feminists, and potential feminists were more supportive than feminists.[26] With regard to increased federal spending on health care and education in general, nonfeminists were the least supportive and feminists were the most supportive.[27]

Significant differences are evident in the women's response concerning other federal government policies. When the issue is government-sponsored plans for provision of health insurance, nonfeminists were the least supportive and feminists were the most supportive.[28] On the issue of requiring employers to allow parents up to six months of unpaid leave to spend time with newborn or newly adopted children, 70 percent of both nonfeminists and potential feminists said they believed that decision should be left up to the employer, as did 50 percent of the feminists.[29]

A major problem for employed women with small children is finding quality child care that is affordable. Significant differences exist among women in general with regard to support for federal government provision of child care assistance to low- and middle-income parents. However, a majority of each group in this study said they believed that the government should provide child care assistance: 51 percent of the nonfeminists, 61 percent of the potential feminists, and 77 percent of the feminists.[30]

Abortion Policy

The most significant differences of opinion on policy among women concern the issue of abortion. Tables 4-3 and 4-4 show differences in abortion attitudes among women categorized on the basis of a measure of feminist group consciousness. In 1992, 68 percent of the feminists, 46 percent of the potential feminists, and 25 percent of the nonfeminists said they believed that "by law, a woman should always be able to have an abortion as a matter of personal choice."[31] In 1992, 78 percent of the nonfeminists, 59 per-

TABLE 4-3

Opinion on the Abortion Issue, by Category of Women's Feminist Support, 1972–1980 (percent)

Opinion	1972			1976			1980		
	Non-feminist	Potential Feminist	Feminist	Non-feminist	Potential Feminist	Feminist	Non-feminist	Potential Feminist	Feminist
Should never be permitted	14	5	7	13	8	4	16	6	1
Permit only if the life and health of the woman is in danger	55	43	28	59	44	22	56	44	22
Permit if woman would have difficulty in caring for the child	15	23	19	12	19	20	12	20	16
Should never be forbidden	16	29	46	16	29	54	16	30	60

Source: Calculated from data in the 1952–1990 American National Election Studies Cumulative File.

TABLE 4-4

Opinion on the Abortion Issue, by Category of Women's Feminist Support, 1980–1992 (percent)

Opinion	1980			1984			1988			1992		
	Non-feminist	Potential Feminist	Feminist	Non-feminist	Potential Feminist	Feminist	Non-feminist	Potential Feminist	Feminist	Non-feminist	Potential Feminist	Feminist
Should never be permitted	20	8	2	20	9	5	22	9	5	21	10	5
Permit only in case of rape, incest, or when the woman's life is in danger	43	32	15	40	25	18	42	31	17	40	28	17
Permit for other reasons, but only after need has been established	14	18	17	18	24	16	16	21	14	14	17	10
Matter of personal choice	24	42	66	22	43	60	19	39	64	25	46	68

Source: Calculated from data in the 1952–1990 American National Election Studies Cumulative File and the 1992 American National Election Study.

cent of the potential feminists, and 41 percent of the feminists supported a state law requiring a married woman to inform her husband before she can obtain an abortion.[32] Nonfeminists were most opposed to state government funding of abortions for women who cannot afford them (65 percent against), and feminists were most supportive (64 percent in favor).[33] However, 78 percent of the nonfeminists, 65 percent of the potential feminists, and 48 percent of the feminists supported a policy requiring parental approval before a teenager under the age of 18 can have an abortion.[34]

The proportion of nonfeminists who believe that abortion should never be permitted increased slightly between 1972 and 1992, as did the proportion who believe that abortion should never be forbidden. Potential feminists increased their support for an absolute right to choose, from 29 percent in 1972 to 46 percent in 1992. Feminists also increased their support for the strongest personal choice option (from 46 percent in 1972 to 68 percent in 1992).

Sexual Harassment

The 1992 study revealed that one-third of both the nonfeminists and potential feminists and almost one-half of the feminists believe that sexual harassment of women in the workplace is a very serious problem.[35] Moreover, one-quarter of the nonfeminists, two-fifths of the potential feminists, and three-fifths of the feminists reported that they or someone they know had been sexually harassed in the workplace.[36] A majority of both nonfeminists and potential feminists and three-fourths of the feminists said they thought too little is being done to protect women from sexual harassment in the workplace.[37] When asked, "if a woman says she has been sexually harassed at work and the man denies it, would you be more likely to believe the woman or the man?" 53 percent of the nonfeminists, 60 percent of the potential feminists, and 68 percent of the feminists reported they would be more likely to believe the woman. An extremely small proportion reported they would be inclined to believe the man.[38]

ASSESSING THE POLITICAL IMPLICATIONS OF DIFFERENCES IN POLICY PREFERENCES

Men and women also differ significantly in their policy preferences on a number of issues; women also differ among themselves. Many of these differences have persisted over time. Although the differences on some issues are not large, they are nevertheless important. If these preferential differences are communicated to public officials, the impact on policy making, implementation, and enforcement can be significant.

Equally as important as policy direction, but infrequently or inadequately measured in many surveys, is the salience of policies—the relative importance of concern with the policy. For example, the availability, quality, and cost of child care facilities is of greater salience to employed parents of two small children than to an employed person with no children. The intensity of policy preferences is also infrequently measured. Some individuals may consider a policy important but they do not have intense feelings about it; others for whom the policy is also important may feel very strongly about it. The latter individuals are more likely to engage in political activity aimed at persuading other citizens and policy makers to adopt the activists' policy preferences. Both pro-life and pro-choice activists find the abortion issue very salient and have very intense feelings about it. Unfortunately, the unavailability of survey data with which to measure policy saliency and the intensity of policy preferences with regard to the issues examined here makes difficult any prediction of the implications for political action.

When differences in policy preferences among women are evaluated on the basis of a measure of feminist group consciousness, they are found to be quite significant on some issues. Women also differ in their beliefs about how best to solve the problems that are perceived as affecting women's status. In 1992, women were asked how women as a group might best improve their status. Two alternatives were presented: (1) each woman should attempt to become better trained and more qualified; and (2) women should work together. Sixty-three percent of the women responding to that question said they thought women need to work together.[39]

Some of the gender differences in political orientation and the differences among women based on their feminist orientation are not as large as those revealed when the data are analyzed on the basis of other characteristics, such as marital status, income, religion, and place of residence. An argument can be made that differences in vote choice are greater when the focus is on marital status, income grouping, or place of residence (urban or rural) than when gender alone is studied.[40]

Chapter 5 seeks answers to several questions not posed here. Do men and women engage in different types of political activities? Do they differ in the extent of their political participation? Are feminists more likely to be politically active than nonfeminists? Do all women participate in the same kinds of political activities, or do their activities differ according to feminist type? What is the likelihood that women can work together to find possible solutions to some of the policy problems discussed in this chapter?

NOTES

1. See Elizabeth Adell Cook, "Measuring Feminist Consciousness," *Women and Politics* 9, no. 3 (1989):71–88; Ethel Klein, *Gender Politics* (Cambridge: Harvard University Press, 1984); Patricia Gurin, "Women's Gender Consciousness," *Public Opinion Quarterly* 49 (1985); Patricia Gurin, Arthur H. Miller, and Gerald Gurin, "Stratum Identification and Consciousness," *Social Psychology Quarterly* 43 (1980); Arthur H. Miller et al., "Group Consciousness and Political Participation," *American Journal of Political Science* 25 (1981); and Sue Tolleson-Rinehart, *Gender Consciousness and Politics.*

2. Tolleson-Rinehart, *Gender Consciousness and Politics* (New York: Routledge, 1992), chaps. 3 and 4.

3. Cook, "Measuring Feminist Consciousness."

4. 1952–1990 American National Election Studies Cumulative File Codebook, variable 834.

5. Gregory B. Markus, "Stability and Change in Political Attitudes: Observed, Recalled, and 'Explained'," *Political Behavior* 8 (1986): 21–44. The data were drawn from a three-wave panel study of high school seniors and their parents who were interviewed in 1965, 1973, and 1982.

6. Claire K. Fulenwider, *Feminism in American Politics: A Study of Ideological Influence* (New York: Praeger, 1980).

7. Tolleson-Rinehart, *Gender Consciousness,* Table 3.2, 55; 1992 American National Election Study, variable 6213. In 1992, 44 percent of the women responding to the survey said they felt close to women and 14 percent said they felt close to feminists (variable 6207). However, 10 percent of the women said that, of the fifteen groups listed, they felt closest to women; only 1 percent said they felt closest to feminists (variable 6218). In response to another survey item, 27 percent said they thought of themselves as feminists (variable 6002), and of those women, 44 percent said they considered themselves to be strong feminists (variable 6003).

8. Calculated from data in the 1952–1990 American National Election Studies Cumulative File, variable 225; 1992 American National Election Study, variable 5317 (feminists).

9. 1992 American National Election Study, variable 5324.

10. Problems exist with these measures of feminist consciousness, regardless of whether they are based on the feeling of closeness to women or on the feeling ther-

mometer evaluations of the women's liberation movement, feminists, or the women's movement. But such measures are the best available for use over several decades and for national samples. The term "women's liberation movement" is rarely used today. In 1988, the American National Election Study substituted for it the term "feminists." That term has a negative connotation for many women, even though they respond positively to the issue concerns and policy agenda of the women's liberation movement. In 1992, the feeling thermometers measured affective orientations toward both "feminists" and the "women's movement." For a discussion of the problem and scales designed to measure the four elements of women's gender consciousness, see Kenneth W. Mease, "Group Consciousness, Social Movements, and Political Participation," Ph.D. diss., University of Florida, 1995.

11. Tolleson-Rinehart (*Gender Consciousness and Politics,* 45) asserts that it is incorrect to divide those who are gender conscious into two groups based on their positive or negative evaluations of the "women's liberation movement." She argues that "consciousness is fundamentally cognitive, not affective, and it is a process, not an endorsement. Those who *are* gender conscious might certainly form attitudes toward the Women's Movement. . . , but such attitudes should be seen as a possible result of consciousness, and not of gender consciousness itself. To put it another way, a gender conscious women would see the Women's Movement as a *means* (or block) to the overarching policy ends her consciousness constrains her to take—but she might not."

12. The women were given the following instructions: "Here is a list of groups. Please read over the list of groups and tell me the letter for those groups you feel particularly close to—people who are most like you in their ideas and interests and feelings about things." Then each respondent was asked: "Of the groups you just mentioned, which one do you feel closest to?" See 1992 American National Election Studies Codebook, variables 6201 and 6218.

13. Tolleson-Rinehart, *Gender Consciousness and Politics,* Table 3.2, 55. Her analysis, covering the period 1972–1988, was based on data from the 1972, 1976, 1980, 1984, and 1988 American National Election Studies and the 1992 American National Election Study.

14. Ibid., Tables 3.8 and 3.9, 61.

15. The term "privatized" was used in this context by Virginia Sapiro in *Political Integration of Women* (Urbana: University of Illinois Press, 1983), 30–31; see Tolleson-Rinehart, *Gender Consciousness and Politics,* chap. 5.

16. Tolleson-Rinehart, *Gender Consciousness and Politics,* Table 4.1, 79.

17. Ibid., 80–81; see also chaps. 4, 5, and 6.

18. Roberta S. Sigel, "Female Perspectives of Gender Relations." Paper presented at the annual meeting of the Midwest Political Science Association, Chicago, April 1988, cited in ibid., 46–47.

19. Cook, in "Measuring Feminist Consciousness," 77–80, makes a strong argument for using the feeling thermometer measure rather than the closeness

measure to evaluate feminist consciousness, claiming that the feeling thermometer measure is adequate and accurate in meaning. She reports that the equal role measure also correlates more strongly with the feeling thermometer measure than with the closeness measure. The data used were collected from a national sample taken in 1976. In a factor analysis of the feeling thermometer scores, those for the women's liberation movement, measures of discontent, system blaming or withdrawal of legitimacy, collective orientation, and the equal role for women item all loaded on the same factor in a principal components analysis. The feeling thermometer measure was more strongly linked to other measures of feminist consciousness than was the closeness measure.

20. Cook, "Measuring Feminist Consciousness," 77.

21. It should be noted that because different labels are used in the analysis, trends are best measured in a time frame in which the measure is based on the same label.

22. Age categories (in years) used in the analysis were: 18 to 27 (generation X), 28 to 37 (younger baby boomers), 38 to 46 (older baby boomers), 47 to 62, 63 to 70, 71 to 83, and older than 83.

23. Prior research using other measures of feminist orientation suggests that political attitudes vary with gender role orientation. Elizabeth Adell Cook, Ted G. Jelen, and Clyde Wilcox, using data from the General Social Survey, developed two measures of gender role orientation: public aspects of gender roles, based on questions about the appropriate role orientations for women in government and business; and private aspects of gender roles, based on individuals' views of the appropriate role orientations for women, such as wife and mother. Attitudes concerning a number of policy issues varied with the feminism measures based on private and public gender role orientations. Attitudes toward abortion also varied with attitudes regarding the desirability of having children, female employment, and sexual morality. See Elizabeth Adell Cook, Ted G. Jelen, and Clyde Wilcox, *Between Two Absolutes: Public Opinion and the Politics of Abortion* (Boulder, Colo.: Westview Press, 1992), Tables 3.3–3.6, 79–84.

24. 1992 American National Election Study, variables 3745, 3815, 3816, 3726, 3730, 3818, and 3819.

25. Ibid., variables 3814, 3817, and 3728.

26. Ibid., variables 3603 and 3707.

27. Ibid., variable 3701.

28. Ibid., variable 3716.

29. Ibid., variable 3717.

30. Ibid., variable 3745.

31. Ibid., variable 3734.

32. Ibid., variable 3740.

33. Ibid., variable 3738.

34. Ibid., variable 3736.

35. Ibid., variable 3741.
36. Ibid., variable 3742.
37. Ibid., variable 3743.
38. Ibid., variable 3744.
39. Ibid., variable 6004.
40. Richard L. Berke, "Voting Differences by Sex Are Overplayed, Study Says," *New York Times,* August 24, 1995, B15. The study's research was sponsored by the National Women's Political Caucus.

SUGGESTIONS FOR FURTHER READING

Collins, Patricia Hill. *Black Feminist Thought: Knowledge, Consciousness, and the Politics of Empowerment.* New York: Routledge, 1991.

Held, Virginia. *Feminist Morality: Transforming Culture, Society, and Politics.* Chicago: University of Chicago Press, 1993.

Kelly, Rita Mae, and Jayne Burgess. "Gender and the Meaning of Power and Politics," *Women and Politics* 9, no. 1 (1989): 47–82.

Tolleson-Rinehart, Sue. *Gender Consciousness and Politics.* New York: Routledge, 1992.

CHAPTER 5

Women's Political Participation

All women citizens of voting age in the United States who met other eligibility criteria, such as length of residence in the state, were guaranteed the right to vote in all elections by the Nineteenth Amendment to the Constitution, ratified by the requisite number of states in August 1920. Prior to 1920, women could participate in politics in ways other than voting, and many did—for example, as part of the women's suffrage movement. Many women did not vote in the first few elections held after women's suffrage was established; either they believed politics was not women's business, or their husbands opposed their participation. Those women who came of voting age after 1920 were more likely to vote than were older women. The Lee family illustrates the evolution of women's political participation. Anna Lee did not vote in the 1920s because her husband, George, did not approve of women voting. However, Anna's daughter Barbara cast her first vote in the statewide election of 1920. Anna's granddaughter Carol became active in her political party's local organization in the 1940s. As a result of her continued work for the party, Carol was elected to the county party organization's executive committee and was later chosen as a delegate to the national party convention. Carol's daughter Donna, a schoolteacher, was elected to the local school board for two consecutive terms, after which she won a seat on the party's county council. When the incumbent state officeholder retired, she sought and won election to a statewide elective office. In four generations, the political participation of this family's women had progressed from voting abstention to election to state office.

Women can now participate fully in political activities, but do they? Do men and women differ in their patterns of political activity? If so, how can these patterns of political activity be explained? This chapter examines patterns of participation in campaigns and elections, as well as in other types of political activity by those who are not members of the political elite.[1]

The term "political activity" as used here includes all types of action that attempt to influence, either directly or indirectly, what governments do: voting; contacting public officials; joining organizations that seek to influence executives, legislators, bureaucrats, and judges; and, less frequently, participating in strikes, boycotts, and protest demonstrations, or marches. Activity intended to influence government policies also includes involvement in professional, social, or community organizations. For example, a sports fishermen's association attempts to pressure the water resources agency concerning policies affecting the quality of fishing in local lakes and rivers; a homeowners' association lobbies the zoning board on decisions affecting the neighborhood; and a parent-teachers organization focuses on obtaining more funding for the schools.

PATTERNS OF POLITICAL PARTICIPATION

Changes in the life circumstances of a substantial proportion of American women since the late 1970s have resulted in increased rates of political participation. More women are now employed outside the home. A larger proportion of women than men now attend college and obtain a college degree. Both increased employment and higher levels of educational attainment are associated with increased rates of political participation.[2]

Those who participate are more likely to have the resources that facilitate participation—time, money, skills, and knowledge—and to have positive attitudes and beliefs. These may contribute either to self-mobilization to political action or to mobilization by others. For example, higher levels of education usually enhance the skills necessary for participation and lead to the acquisition of other resources, such as knowledge, verbal skills, and money or social status, which facilitate participation.

TABLE 5-1

Gender Differences in Voter Turnout in Presidential Elections, 1964–1992 (percent)

Year	Men	Women
1964	72	67
1968	70	66
1972	64	62
1976	60	59
1980	59	59
1984	59	61
1988	56	58
1992	60	62

Source: U.S. Department of Commerce, Bureau of the Census, Current Population Reports, *Voting and Registration in the Election of November, 1992,* Series P-20, no. 466, Table A.

Voting

Initially, women's rate of voter turnout was lower than expected and continued to be lower than that of men until 1980.[3] Voter turnout has been higher among women than among men in every presidential election since 1984 (see Table 5-1). Cheryl Christy examined change in voter turnout in the United States and other modern democracies over a thirty-six year period and the variables believed to impact on rates of voter participation. She found a gradual decrease in gender differences in voter turnout rates.[4] Changes in social norms and electoral laws have eliminated or reduced a number of factors that once inhibited women's voting participation. To the extent that gender differences in voter turnout rates now exist, they tend to be affected by variables related to issues and candidate characteristics, which vary from election to election. In the United States not only are women now more likely than men to vote in presidential elections, but a gender gap is evident in party choice.[5]

A higher percentage of women than men have cast their votes for Democratic candidates in presidential elections since 1980. This pattern is evident among voters of all age groups and educational attainment levels. The gender gap is greatest among the most educated and the least educated voters, however, suggesting that it has many possible explanations. For

TABLE 5-2

Gender Differences in Voter Turnout in Midterm Congressional Elections, 1966–1994 (percent)

Year	Men	Women
1966	58	53
1970	57	53
1974	46	43
1978	47	45
1982	49	48
1986	46	46
1990	45	45
1994	45	45

Sources: U.S. Department of Commerce, Bureau of the Census, Current Population Reports, *Voting and Registration in the Election of November, 1986,* Series P-20, no. 414, Table A; *Voting and Registration in the Election of November, 1990,* Series P-20, no. 453, Table C. 1994 data were obtained from http://www.census.gov/population/socdemo/voting/profile/pttable1.dat.

the former, it may reflect perceptions of economic interests. For the latter, it may reflect a greater awareness of the Democratic Party's support for equal opportunities for women and for government activism in solving problems related to social and educational policy. In 1992, for example, the major concern of women with less than a high school education was the economy and their children's economic future. College-educated women focused not only on the economy but also on the presidential candidates' positions on the abortion issue. A slight voter bias against women candidates for elective office was evident in 1970. (13 percent of the voters queried would not vote for a "qualified" woman candidate.) The proportion opposed to a woman candidate had declined to 6 percent by 1984. (For a more extensive discussion of the gender gap among voters, see Chapter 3.)

Other Forms of Political Activity

In the 1960s women were less likely than men to vote and also less likely to engage in other forms of political activity. For example, in 1960 only college-educated women participated in political activity (defined as attending school board or city council meetings and contacting local officials) to the same extent as college-educated men. By 1976, women with

TABLE 5-3

Gender Differences in Types of Political Participation, 1994 (percent)

Activity	Men	Women
Signed petition	47	49
Attended a public meeting on town or school affairs	40	45
Attended a political rally or speech	20	27
Wrote to congressional or state representative	26	34

Source: Roper Center Survey for *Reader's Digest,* reported in *Public Perspective* 6, no. 3 (April/May, 1995): 23.

a high school education were as likely to participate in these local activities as men with a high school education.[6] In 1994, women were more likely than men to report having signed a petition. They were more likely than men to have attended a public meeting of a local government agency or school board, attended a political speech or rally, or written to a member of Congress or a state legislator (see Table 5-3).

To determine whether women are more likely than men to participate in campaign activities, we can examine survey respondents' reports of participation in five types of campaign activities: working for a candidate or political party, contributing money, attending a political meeting or a campaign rally, trying to persuade someone else how to vote, and wearing a campaign button or displaying a campaign sticker.[7] Figure 5-1 shows the proportions of men and women who reported participating in at least one of these campaign activities during presidential election campaigns from 1952 to 1992. It suggests that women are less likely to report participating in any of these campaign activities than are men. As a second measure, we can combine the reports of participation in these five activities to obtain the total number of campaign activities of each individual and create an index which ranges from zero (engaging in no campaign activities) to 5 (engaging in all five types of activities). We find that in ten of the eleven presidential election campaigns from 1952 to 1992, women engaged in fewer campaign activities than did men.[8]

One reason why people participate in politics is because they are asked. Men are more likely to be asked to give money than are women. In 1992 men were contacted more frequently than women, both in person and by phone and mail, with requests to make campaign contributions. As a consequence, men were more likely than women to report making contributions.[9]

FIGURE 5-1

Participation of Men and Women in at Least One Campaign Activity, Presidential Elections of 1952–1992

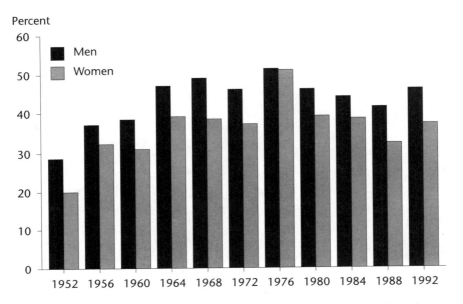

Source: Calculated from data in the 1952–1992 American National Election Studies Cumulative File.

Beginning in the 1980s, several groups affiliated with each of the two major parties made substantial efforts to increase women's campaign contributions to candidates and especially to women candidates. These organizations focus on candidates for the House of Representatives and the Senate as well as on candidates for major statewide and local offices. Two of the most prominent such organizations are partisan—Emily's List, which supports Democratic candidates, and the Wish List, which supports Republican candidates. Others are affiliated with a professional association, such as the political action committee (PAC) associated with the American Nurses Association. The number of PACs focusing on women candidates at the federal level increased dramatically during the last quarter of the twentieth century. In 1976 only 4 such PACs existed; in 1992, 45 registered with the Federal Election Commission and 29 made contributions to women candidates for federal office.[10] In 1996, 55 PACs and donor networks either supported mostly women candidates or raised money primarily by soliciting contributions from women. Nine of those groups operated at the national level; 37 focused on particular states.[11]

These women's PACs have significantly increased the amount of money that women give to political candidates. Women's PACs contributed $11.5 million to women candidates for office in 1992, compared with $1.1 million in 1988. Their support also increases the ability of women candidates to raise sufficient funds to be competitive in contests for local, state, and national offices.[12] Several studies conclude that, after taking into account the type of contest (open seat as compared with incumbent-challenger) and the partisan nature of the district, women are not disadvantaged in raising funds to run for the House of Representatives.[13] Other research focusing on local elections suggests that women are more likely to give to women candidates than to men candidates.[14]

Focusing on explicitly political activity may ignore important forms of participation in community activities, which provide an opportunity to develop leadership and communications skills that can be used in political activity. Community activities may also serve as a means for the acquisition of politically relevant information and facilitate informal communication with community leaders. A longitudinal study of Americans who were first interviewed as high school seniors in 1972 provides evidence of different patterns of community and political participation among men and women. When interviewed in 1972, the women were more likely to be active in and assume a leadership role in high school activities than were the men. When these members of the "baby boomer" generation were reinterviewed in 1986, there were significant gender differences in terms of membership in community organizations. Men were significantly more likely to be members of union, farm, and professional organizations, sports teams or clubs, and service organizations. Women were more likely to be members of youth, religious, and educational or academic organizations. A similar pattern is evident with regard to active participation. When we consider the total number of activities in which each of these baby boomers was a member, we find that women were slightly more likely to be members of, and active participants in, more community organizations.[15]

But the patterns of community organization membership and activity of these baby boomers did not translate into political participation. Men were more likely than women to report trying to persuade others to vote for a particular candidate, to contribute money to campaigns, to attend political gatherings, and to have held political or governmental office. Men were also more likely to report sometimes or frequently talking about political problems with friends, co-workers, community leaders, and elected officials.[16]

A national survey conducted in 1990 that focused on political participation provides additional evidence that women are less politically active than men. Women were less likely to contribute to political campaigns, to work informally in the community, to serve on a local governing board, to contact a government official, or to be affiliated with a political organization. When the eight possible types of political participation are combined to obtain an index of participation ranging from zero to 8, women are found to have a lower average political participation score than men.[17]

To what extent are women willing to engage in less conventional forms of political participation? A 1974 study reports that women of all age groups are less supportive than men of unconventional political action, or protest.[18] Data from other studies confirm this finding and suggest that support for protest activities is a function of the social and political context. During the Vietnam War (1968–1974), disapproval of protest meetings, sit-ins, and antiwar demonstrations decreased as the war became more unpopular. The proportion of men disapproving of protest activities decreased from 74 percent in 1968 to 62 percent in 1974; the proportion of women disapproving decreased from 77 percent in 1968 to 59 percent in 1974.[19]

EXPLANATIONS FOR PATTERNS OF POLITICAL PARTICIPATION

Patterns of political participation are influenced by the extent to which individuals have the resources that facilitate participation, their social status, their motivation to participate, and the legal structure and political environment, all of which can either facilitate or inhibit participation.[20] Resources that facilitate participation include both educational attainment level and life experiences, which can substitute for or supplement the learning acquired through formal education. Social status may be conferred by personal achievement or by group membership (in social, service, and religious organizations). Certain attitudes, such as a sense of moral obligation to participate in politics, an empowering sense of personal political efficacy, loyal commitment to a candidate or political party, concern about a policy issue or set of issues, and the social context (including pressures to participate that may exist in any social status group) may stimulate both social and political involvement—that is, interest in and attention to politics and public policy and concern with the outcome of political processes. Individuals may also be motivated to participate as a result of the efforts of candidates, political parties, social and political movements, and interest groups. Participation in elections may be increased or decreased by voter eligibility requirements and by the administrative processes, such as voter registration procedures, that regulate the electoral process. The political environment also affects patterns of participation. For example, in some localities women are encouraged to be candidates for elective office, whereas in others, local political elites discourage women from running for office.

Educational Attainment Level

Both historical and current patterns of political participation are partly explained by differences in educational attainment level. Those with more education generally know more about the political system and have a better understanding of how government policies affect their lives. They are also more likely to believe that their political activities can change policy outcomes. Peer pressures to participate are generally greater in the social environment of such individuals. Social norms in both the parental family and the adult peer group of those with higher levels of educational attainment contribute to the pressure to participate at least to the extent of voting. Education also provides skills in the acquisition, processing, and analysis of information that facilitate the making of judgments about courses of political action more consistent with individual interests.[21] Those with more education are also likely to have more skill in dealing with bureaucracies, which was a necessary part of the voter registration process prior to the implementation in 1995 of the federal "motor voter" law, which greatly facilitated that process.[22] Those with more education are likely to be more interested in politics and to consume more intelligently the print news media's coverage of government and politics.[23] Experiences in educational institutions or religious institutions and social or service clubs can contribute to the acquisition of the resources and skills necessary for successful participation in some more demanding forms of political activity, such as working for a political party or with an interest group, or running for office.[24] Educational attainment varies with age; younger individuals tend to have higher levels of educational attainment.

Gender differences in voting participation vary with educational attainment. In the 1992 presidential election, voter trunout was generally higher among women age 54 and younger than among men age 54 and younger. The reverse pattern was evident among those age 55 and older; men were more likely to vote than women. However, educational attainment interacts with age in affecting voting participation. Among those age 54 and younger, women were more likely to vote than men in each category of educational attainment. But among citizens age 65 or older, men were more likely to vote than women in each category of educational attainment. In the intermediate age group (ages 55 to 64), voter turnout was lower among women with less than a high school education than among men with comparable levels of education, but women with a high school education or more had higher voting participation rates than did men with comparable levels of education.

Type of Employment

Type of employment has a significant effect on patterns of political participation. Women who work outside the home tend to participate in politics more than those who do not. In 1992, 42 percent of the women and 55 percent of the men who were employed outside the home participated in at least one campaign activity compared with only 32 percent of the women and 45 percent of the men who were not employed.[25]

There are several possible explanations for the political participation of women employed outside the home. They may have greater exposure to communications about how government policies affect their interests and pressure from co-workers or employers to participate. Women employed outside the home may also more directly experience the effects of federal, state, and local government policies requiring non-discrimination in education, employment, training, and promotion.[26]

Political Involvement

One explanation for men's higher rate of campaign activity is their much higher level of political involvement, or interest in and attention to what happens in government and politics. Men are more likely than women to report that they follow what is going on in politics, care a good deal about who wins elections, and are interested in campaigns. Despite this gender difference, women are now more likely to vote than are men. However, women are less likely to participate in campaigns and in some other types of political activity such as contacting public officials (see Tables 5-3 and 5-4).

TABLE 5-4

Gender Differences in Political Involvement, Presidential Elections of 1952–1992 (percent)

Year	Interested in the Campaign		Care a Good Deal Who Wins the Election		Follow Politics Some or Most of the Time	
	Men	Women	Men	Women	Men	Women
1952	40	34	69	65	—	—
1956	34	26	66	61	—	—
1960	42	34	68	63	71	54
1964	40	36	66	66	70	66
1968	44	35	66	64	71	58
1972	37	27	61	60	80	68
1976	41	34	58	56	78	64
1980	33	27	56	56	69	55
1984	33	25	66	64	68	59
1988	32	25	64	59	69	52
1992	42	36	76	76	74	62

Source: Calculated from data in the 1952–1990 American National Election Studies Cumulative File and the 1992 American National Election Study.

A commitment to a political party and concern with its success in gaining election of its candidates to office can motivate involvement. One measure of this commitment is strength of party identification. The expectation is that those who more strongly identify themselves as a party member will be more likely to vote and to participate in campaigns. Women do not differ significantly from men in the strength of party identification. However, as previously mentioned, women are more likely than men to identify with the Democratic Party.

Political participation is affected by political attitudes and beliefs. Those who believe that they can be politically effective and that the government is responsive to voters' concerns are more likely to participate by voting and participating in campaigns. One aspect of this belief is the perception that public officials care about the opinions of individuals like oneself. In 1992, women were less likely to have this perception. That indicates a lower level of external political efficacy, but it also reflects past patterns of public policy, in which women's concerns and policy needs have received less attention from (mostly male) public officials.[27] Internal political efficacy includes a belief that politics and government are not too complicated to understand

TABLE 5-5

Women's Reported Voter Turnout, by Level of Feminist Consciousness, Presidential Elections of 1972–1992 (percent)

Year	None	Potential	Feminist
1972	67	78	82
1976	69	76	76
1980	66	74	74
1984	71	80	78
1988	69	72	74
1992a	73	78	81
1992b	74	79	81

Source: Based in part on response to feeling thermometer measures evaluating the women's liberation movement (1972 to 1984), feminists (1988 and 1992a), and the women's movement (1992b). Calculated from data in the 1952–1990 American National Election Studies Cumulative File and the 1992 American National Election Study.

and a confidence that one understands the important national issues and is well qualified to participate in politics. In 1992, women as a group were found to have less sense of internal political efficacy than men.[28]

Social Circumstances

The resources and opportunities to participate also vary with the individuals' social circumstances. One crucial resource is time. Voting turnout among men does not vary with the number of children in the household. In contrast, the more children in the household, the less likely women are to vote. In 1992, 80 percent of women with no children in the household reported having voted, compared with 76 percent of the women who had one child under the age of 18 living at home, 73 percent with two children, 71 percent with three children, and 57 percent with four or more children living at home.[29]

Women have fewer of any of the resources (time, money, and skills) that facilitate political participation. Women are less likely than men to work outside the home; women who do tend to be employed in occupations that do not facilitate the acquisition or exercise of politically relevant skills. Furthermore, women's incomes tend to be lower; in a two-income family, the proportion contributed by the woman tends to be less. Women's participation in religious and voluntary organizations constitutes an alternative resource for political participation (by facilitating the development of participatory skills) that partially offsets the advantages accruing to men as a result of their higher levels of education and income, and their advantage in terms of job skills.[30]

FEMINIST CONSCIOUSNESS AND PATTERNS
OF POLITICAL PARTICIPATION

Women's political participation seems to vary with their level of feminist consciousness.[31] As Table 5-5 indicates, those who are feminists or have the potential to become feminists tend to have higher rates of voter turnout than those who are not feminists. In three of the six presidential elections held between 1972 and 1992, the most significant difference was between those who were not feminists (the "None" category) and those who were.

FIGURE 5-2

Participation of Women in at Least One Campaign Activity, by Level of Feminist Consciousness, Presidential Elections of 1972–1992

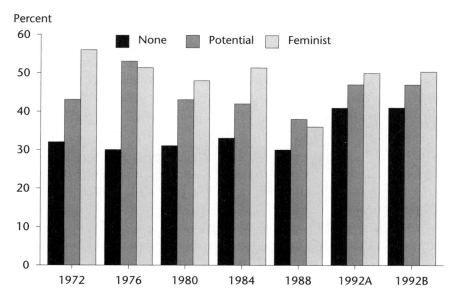

Source: Calculated from data in the 1952–1992 American National Election Studies Cumulative File.

Note: The measure of feminism in 1992A is calculated using evaluations of feminists. The measure in 1992B is calculated using evaluations of the women's movement.

TABLE 5-6
Women's Political Involvement, by Level of Feminist Consciousness, Presidential Elections of 1972–1992 (percent)

Year	Very Interested in the Campaign			Care Very Much Who Wins			Follow Politics Some or Most of the Time			Presidential Election Outcome Will Be Close		
	None	Potential	Feminist	None	Potential	Feminist	None	Potential	Feminist	None	Potential	Feminist
1972	27	39	43	60	62	61	69	83	84	32	31	34
1976	35	44	41	57	58	53	68	76	77	68	76	76
1980	27	32	37	53	55	54	58	65	67	67	72	74
1984	26	30	40	65	65	70	60	66	73	47	45	52
1988	30	29	35	60	64	69	68	61	66	69	70	76
1992	33	38	41	74	78	80	—	—	—	—	—	—

Source: Calculated from data in the 1952–1992 American National Election Studies Cumulative File.

Women who were classified as feminists were also more likely to engage in campaign activities in four of the six presidential elections studied, and in all six elections both feminists and potential feminists were significantly more likely to engage in campaign activities than were nonfeminists (see Figure 5-2). Feminists' attitudes and beliefs about the political system often differed from those of nonfeminists and potential feminists. In 1984 and 1988, feminists tended to be more interested than non- and potential feminists in the election campaign and to follow politics more closely, but they did not express more concern about who would win the election (see Table 5-6). Potential feminists were more likely to believe that public officials care what people like them think and in 1972 were more likely to believe that elections make the government pay attention to what citizens want.

Women are now politically active citizens, and their rates of voting in elections are equal to (and in presidential elections, greater than) those of men. However, women are less likely to engage in campaign activities, and when they do, they engage in fewer campaign activities than men. Women have just as much or more of one of the crucial resources—education—that promotes political participation. However, they are not as likely to have equivalent amounts of other resources that are associated with higher levels of participation, such as personal income, occupations that facilitate political participation, and a sense of political efficacy.

Patterns of group consciousness have changed significantly since 1972. Fewer women now accept the view that women's place is in the home and more believe that women should play an equal role with men in business, industry, and government. More women now report a positive evaluation of the women's movement and consider themselves to be close to other women, although fewer women give equally positive evaluations to feminists or select women as the group to which they feel closest. An index score of feminist consciousness reveals differences between feminists and nonfeminists in both voter turnout and other forms of political activity. Feminists also differ from nonfeminists in two measures of political involvement—interest in the campaign, and (in some years) following politics some or most of the time.

NOTES

1. "Political elite" refers collectively to persons holding an elective or appointive office in a local or state government or in the federal government.

2. See Sandra Baxter and Marjorie Lansing, *Women and Politics: The Invisible Majority* (Ann Arbor: University of Michigan Press, 1980); Karen Beckwith, *American Women and Political Participation* (New York: Greenwood Press, 1986); M. Margaret Conway, *Political Participation in the United States,* 2d ed. (Washington, D.C.: CQ Press, 1991); Raymond E. Wolfinger and Steven J. Rosenstone, *Who Votes?* (New Haven, Conn.: Yale University Press, 1980); Steven J. Rosenstone and John Mark Hansen, *Mobilization, Participation, and Democracy in America* (New York: Macmillan, 1993); and Ruy A. Teixeira, *The Disappearing American Voter* (Washington, D.C.: Brookings Institution, 1992).

3. Martin Gruberg, *Women in American Politics* (Oshkosh, Wis.: Academica Press, 1968), 9.

4. Cheryl Christy, "Trends in Sex Differences in Political Participation: A Comparative Perspective," in Marianne Githens, Pippa Norris, and Joni Lovenduski, eds., *Different Voices, Different Roles* (New York: HarperCollins, 1994), 27–37.

5. See Sue Tolleson-Rinehart and Kenneth Hanses, "Gendered Parties, Partisan Gender Roles: The Four Groups Who Cause the Gender Gap, 1980–1988." Paper presented at the 1992 meeting of the Midwest Political Science Association; Mary E. Bendyna and Celinda C. Lake, "Gender and Voting in the 1992 Presidential Election," in Elizabeth Adell Cook, Sue Thomas, and Clyde Wilcox, *The Year of the Woman: Myths and Realities* (Boulder, Colo.: Westview Press, 1994), 236–254. See also Carole Chaney and Barbara Sinclair, "Women and the 1992 House Elections," in Cook, Thomas, and Wilcox, *Year of the Woman,* 123–139.

6. Nancy McGlen and Karen O'Connor, *Women's Rights* (New York: Praeger, 1983), 105–106.

7. Calculated from data in the 1952–1992 American National Election Studies Cumulative File.

8. Ibid.

9. Calculated from data in the 1992 American National Election Study. In 1992, 8.9 percent of the men reported making a political contribution, compared with 5.6 percent of the women. The difference is statistically significant ($p = .0064$).

10. Susan Roberts, "Furthering Feminism and Female Representation: The Role of Women's PACs in Recruitment." Paper presented at the 1993 meeting of the Midwest Political Science Association, Chicago. In 1992, 42 PACs either gave money predominantly to women or had a donor base composed largely of women.

11. Center for the American Woman and Politics, Eagleton Institute of Politics, Rutgers University, "Women's PACs in 1990: Continuing to Make a Difference,"

News and Notes 9 (1993): 10 and 10 (winter 1996): 6; cited in Chaney and Sinclair, "Women and the 1992 House Elections," 130.

12. Candice J. Nelson, "Women's PACs in the Year of the Woman," in Cook, Thomas, and Wilcox, *Year of the Woman,* 181–195.

13. Chaney and Sinclair, "Women and the 1992 House Elections," 128; Barbara Burrell, *A Woman's Place Is in the House* (Ann Arbor: University of Michigan Press, 1994), chap. 6; Joanne Marie Connor, "Dynamics of Open Seat Elections for the United States House of Representatives" (Ph.D. diss., University of Florida, 1994); and Carole J. Uhlaner and Kay Lehman Schlozman, "Candidate Gender and Congressional Campaign Receipts," *Journal of Politics* 48 (1984): 30–50.

14. Gerald Ingalls and Theodore S. Arrington, "The Role of Gender in Local Campaign Financing: The Case of Charlotte, North Carolina," *Women and Politics* 11 (1991): 61–89.

15. Calculated from data in U.S. Department of Education, Office of Educational Research and Improvement, "National Longitudinal Study of the High School Class of 1972" (Washington, D.C.: National Center for Educational Statistics).

16. Ibid.

17. Kay Lehman Schlozman, Nancy Burns, and Sidney Verba, "Gender and Pathways to Participation: The Role of Resources," *Journal of Politics* 56 (November 1994): 963–990.

18. Alan Marsh and Max Kaase, "Background of Political Action," in Samuel H. Barnes and Max Kaase, *Political Action* (Beverly Hills, Calif.: Sage Publications, 1979), Table 4.2, 108.

19. Calculated from data in the 1952–1990 American National Election Studies Cumulative File, variable 642.

20. Sidney Verba, Kay Lehman Schlozman, and Henry E. Brady, *Voice and Equality* (Cambridge: Harvard University Press, 1995).

21. See Gabriel Almond and Sidney Verba, *The Civic Culture* (Princeton, N.J.: Princeton University Press, 1963), 379–381; Wolfinger and Rosenstone, *Who Votes?* chap. 2; and Conway, *Political Participation in the United States,* 23–25.

22. The "motor voter" law requires all states to make voter registration forms available in state agencies such as the motor vehicle registration bureaus and drivers' licensing agencies. The national voter registration bill was enacted by Congress in May 1993; the law went into effect January 1, 1995.

23. Conway, *Political Participation in the United States,* 13–15.

24. Verba, Schlozman, and Brady, *Voice and Equality,* chap. 11.

25. Calculated from data in the 1992 American National Election Study.

26. See M. Margaret Conway, David W. Ahern, and Gertrude A. Steuernagel, *Women and Public Policy: A Revolution in Progress* (Washington, D.C.: CQ Press, 1995), chap. 4.

27. Calculated from data in the 1952–1990 American National Election Studies Cumulative File and the 1992 American National Election Study. For a discussion of the policy needs of women, see Conway, Ahern, and Steuernagel, *Women and Public Policy.*

28. Calculated from data in the 1992 American National Election Study.

29. Ibid.

30. Schlozman, Burns, and Verba, "Gender and Pathways to Participation," Table 5, 984.

31. For a wide-ranging comparison of gender differences in feminist consciousness, see Ethel Klein, "The Diffusion of Consciousness in the United States and Western Europe," in Mary Fainsod Katzenstein and Carol McClurg Mueller, *The Women's Movements of the United States and Western Europe* (Philadelphia: Temple University Press, 1987), 23–43. For a discussion of gender consciousness, including its sources and consequences in the United States, see Sue Tolleson-Rinehart, *Gender Consciousness and Politics* (New York: Routledge, 1992).

SUGGESTIONS FOR FURTHER READING

Carty, Linda, ed. *And Still We Rise: Feminist Political Mobilizing in Contemporary Canada.* Toronto: Women's Press, 1993.

Darcy, Robert E., Charles D. Hadley, and Jason F. Kirksey. "Election Systems and the Representation of Black Women in American State Legislatures." *Women and Politics* 13, no. 2 (1993): 73–89.

Herrick, Rebekah. "Is There a Gender Gap in the Value of Campaign Resources?" *American Politics Quarterly* 24, no. 1 (January 1996): 68–80.

Lockwood, Victoria S. *Tahitian Transformation: Gender and Capitalist Development in a Rural Society.* Boulder, Colo.: Lynne Rienner, 1993.

Lorber, Judith, and Farrell, Susan A., eds. *The Social Construction of Gender.* Newbury Park, Calif.: Sage Publications, 1991.

Rapoport, Ronald, Walter Stone, and Alan Abramowitz. "Sex and the Caucus Participant: The Gender Gap and Presidential Nominations." *American Journal of Political Science* 515 (May 1991): 23–37.

Rusciano, Frank Louis. "Rethinking the Gender Gap: The Case of West German Elections, 1949–1987." *Comparative Politics* 24, no. 3 (April 1992): 335–357.

Schubert, Glendon A. *Sexual Politics and Political Feminism.* Greenwich, Conn.: JAI Press, 1991.

Small, Lisa. "Presidential Campaign Ignores Women's Issues." *New Directions for Women* 21, no. 3 (May–June 1992): 3.

CHAPTER 6

Opening the Doors to Political Power:
Women as Members of the Political Elite

The nature of women's participation at the highest levels of the political system has changed dramatically since the 1970s. Susan Tolchin and Martin Tolchin have discussed the comments made by Moon Landrieu, mayor of New Orleans (1970–1978), and John V. Lindsay, liberal Republican mayor of New York City (1966–1973), about the roles women played in their respective campaigns and administrations. Most party politicians at that time viewed women as party cheerleaders and campaign workers who performed well the menial tasks associated with secretarial work—stuffing the envelopes, licking the stamps, and distributing campaign literature—but who should not be involved in making strategic political decisions. As Landrieu put it, "Women do the lickin' and the stickin' while men plan the strategy." Mayor Lindsay expressed a similar view; when asked by a woman reporter why there were not more women commissioners in his administration, he replied, "Honey, whatever women do, they do best after dark." Such attitudes led the Tolchins to conclude that

> the very texture of American politics—its folkways and byways—militates against women's entry into the mainstream. The smoke-filled rooms, bourbon and branchwater rites, and all-night poker games exclude women from the fellowship and cronyism that seals the bonds of power. It is an

exclusion practiced by Republicans and Democrats, reformers and regulars, liberals and conservatives. It crosses economic and social barriers, showing little distinction between rich and poor, social lions, the upwardly mobile, and the disinherited. Nor do years of service, party loyalty, wisdom or experience provide women with a passport to those inner circles where priorities are set, careers advanced, and strategies determined.

The late Millicent Fenwick, when serving as a New Jersey state legislator, echoed these sentiments: "Women are on the outside when the door to the smoke-filled room is closed."[1]

The metaphor of the closed door is indeed an appropriate one. For just as doors closed deny access to rooms, doors closed to meaningful participation in politics deny access to political power. In 1973 the doors to political power were effectively closed to women. The comments of Landrieu and Lindsay were not only sexist but reflected the fact that the lack of access to political power would have consequences for women after the elections. Their work for parties and for candidates was not translating into more appointments to positions of influence.

On October 8, 1991, a door again became a symbol of the obstacles that women still had to overcome—this time to gain access to a room in the powerful United States Senate. Barbara Boxer, elected senator from California in 1992, has discussed what became for many a defining moment in the mobilization of women: the possibility that they would be denied participation in a Senate decision on whether to pursue extensive questioning of Supreme Court nominee Clarence Thomas after the accusations of sexual harassment made by University of Oklahoma law professor Anita Hill. Two days after the allegations were made, when it appeared that both the House and Senate were unwilling to devote time to a thorough exploration of the charges, Reps. Patricia Schroeder (D-Colo.), Barbara Boxer (D-Calif.), Eleanor Holmes Norton (D-D.C.), Louise Slaughter (D-N.Y.), Jolene Unsoeld (D-Wash.), Nita Lowey (D-N.Y.), and Patsy Mink (D-Hawaii) walked out of the House of Representatives and over to the Senate. Reporters and photographers followed; the photograph of the seven women marching up the steps of the Senate has been described as "the women's Iwo Jima"—a comparison to the raising of the American flag on the Pacific island during World War II. This action, captured in this photo, made an indelible mark on the public consciousness and came to symbolize something far more profound than the event itself. Boxer explained the women's feelings as follows: "As often happens when people act in synch, there was little talking as we walked. We didn't plan what we would tell the Senators but we knew that we'd tell them the truth about what we were feeling. And we knew that we would be of help to them—and we wanted to be of help; with only two women in the Senate, they could use our perspective. We felt that we would be welcome, or that at least our advice would be welcome." The women went to the room in the Senate where the members of the Democratic caucus were discussing the Thomas nomination, knocked on the door, and were told by a senior congressional aide that they could not come in. They told a female staffer that the reporters who had accompanied them knew why they had come and would certainly be interested to know the outcome. After some delay, the staffer told them that the Senate majority leader would see them in the side room. Boxer has reflected on these events: "The day we knocked on that door was an extraordinary circumstance, as history has shown. The seven of us were the only group of women in the country who could get at all close to where the decision over Clarence Thomas would be made. It's hard for me to explain how it felt for seven grown women, experienced in life and in politics, to have to pound on a closed door, to have to beg to be heard on a crucial issue that couldn't really wait for niceties." A senator later told Boxer that strangers were not allowed in that room; strangers in this context meant non-senators. But for Boxer, "the truth is that women have been strangers in the Senate . . . strangers in the highest, most powerful legislative body in the world."[2]

Boxer's story is relevant to an understanding of the American political system, contemporary political culture, and the changing role that women are playing in American politics. Women are still underrepresented in the halls of power, but they are beginning to make a difference. Although those seven women were unable to stop the selection of Clarence Thomas, they fundamentally raised public consciousness about the issue of sexual harassment. The lack of understanding of the issue demonstrated by the Senate committee, by political commentators, and by the general public incensed many women and spurred them to vote in 1992. The large turnout of women voters helped to unseat an incumbent president and was partly responsible for a nearly twofold increase in the number of women in Congress.

Since the mid-1960s, women have organized caucuses and interest groups such as the National Organization for Women, the National Women's Political Caucus, Emily's List (Early Money Is Like Yeast), and the Congressional Caucus for Women's Issues to effectively lobby for women's concerns, to encourage women to seek elective office, and to support women candidates. Groups have been organized at all levels of government and in all of the institutions in which decisions of relevance to women are made. And women have become increasingly visible as political actors; no longer merely "cheerleaders," they now seek and win elective office and are appointed to positions of power and responsibility in a wide range of political organizations at all levels (local, state, and national) and in all three branches of government (legislative, executive, and judicial).

Most of the success stories in this chapter date from 1973; however, it should be remembered that women enjoyed some success prior to the 1970s. As discussed in Chapter 2, their active participation in and leadership of the dominant social movements of the nineteenth century had a significant impact on public policy, resulting in improved working conditions, increased educational opportunities, and passage of the Thirteenth and Nineteenth Amendments. Many of these social movements provided women the opportunity to exert the leadership that had effectively been denied them in the traditional institutions of political power. Women today are active in similar social movements since many policy concerns are still of interest to them. The changes that have occurred in women's political attitudes and political participation were the subject of Chapters 3 through 5. This chapter explores women's recent successes in opening the doors to opportunities at higher levels of political power, that is, becoming members of the political elite.

WOMEN, POWER, AND THE POLITICAL CULTURE

The small group of individuals who hold high-level positions of power and responsibility in a government is generally referred to as the political elite. They help to shape political values and control governmental resources, thus influencing the politics of the society. Throughout most of the nation's history, women have not been members of the political elite; therefore, the issues of importance to women have been either absent from or at the bottom of the public agenda. Women's more recent advances in gaining political representation (although certainly not in proportion to their numbers) have come in spite of the fact that the political system largely reflects the values of affluent white males. As women increasingly attain leadership positions in political organizations such as the major political parties and in political institutions, they will have an opportunity to change how these institutions operate (as did Barbara Boxer and her six colleagues) and to have a significant impact on public policies, thus ultimately influencing the political culture. Their ability to exert leadership within these various organizations and institutions thus can have dramatic consequences for women specifically and for society in general. Two questions that should be asked at this point are: What is leadership? How is women's political future affected by society's view of leadership?

Gendered Notions of Leadership

The fact that women were long denied access to the avenues of political participation, and that most positions of political power have been held by males, has conditioned society to associate the characteristics of leadership with male behavior. Two frequently cited definitions of politics reflect a male approach to power and politics: politics is about "who gets what, where, when, why and how," and politics is about "the authoritative allocation of values for society"—that is, capturing resources and redistributing them from losers to winners. Is that what politics is really all about? Many observers, such as Nel Noddings, assert that this is clearly a male approach to the notion of politics and power. Perhaps if more women had been leaders throughout history, leadership might be associated with the ability to get individuals and groups to work together to find a common ground. The ability to seek compromise and consensual solutions to problems is often less associated with leadership than is the willingness or ability to exert power. Is the ability to get people to do something they might not otherwise do (exert power over people) a better definition of leadership than one that emphasizes the ability to get people to reason together and to seek compromise (attempt to empower them)? Is there any theory that logically and convincingly equates the use of power or force with leadership, or is this simply the male standard? Noddings suggests that it is; she argues that the establishment of a more egalitarian educational system requires a long-term effort to challenge the male standard that is dominant in education and to replace it with a female standard.[3]

The influence of the male standard is evident in some political pundits' assessments of President Bill Clinton and Hillary Rodham Clinton. Bill Clinton is often criticized for taking too long to make a decision, listening to too many viewpoints, and changing his mind several times before reaching a decision. These are viewed by many as unfavorable characteristics.

Making a decision and sticking with it, choosing a point of view and then fighting for it is considered manly, and presidential. Hillary Rodham Clinton is often criticized from the opposite perspective as being too strong, too power hungry. Political pundits use derogatory titles such as "the Iron Lady" (see Chapter 7), and bumper stickers proclaim "I didn't vote for President Hillary" or "Impeach Clinton (and Her Husband, Too)." Someone who is "made of iron" is considered to be strong or tough, and toughness is a desired attribute in a man (Otto von Bismarck was known as the Iron Chancellor of Prussia), but not in a woman.

There is no universally accepted definition of leadership. Richard Neustadt, one of the most respected scholars of the American presidency, asserts that presidential power is the power to persuade, and the power to persuade is the ability to bargain.[4] Although persuasion is an important mechanism for exerting power and influence, this definition of presidential power certainly does not imply the use of force. Camilla Stivers observes that there have been hundreds of attempts to define the term leadership and that the vagueness of the term and the continued reliance on the term are ideological in two ways: "Leadership is an important cultural myth by which we make sense of and impart significance to organizational and political experience; in addition, leadership is an idea used to support and rationalize the continuation of existing political-economic, racial and gender arrangements."[5] Her insightful comments may explain the difficulties some women encounter when being evaluated for positions of leadership. A specific societal view of leadership has been conditioned by the interpretation of American history as written. A strong leader, whether in business, the military, or politics, attempts to exert his or her will over a situation. This conditions how the public will rate the capabilities of other aspiring leaders. Well-to-do white males have been the titans of business and have dominated the military; many of them have argued that, on the basis of these credentials, they should hold the reins of political power as well. If this view prevailed, of course, it would ensure the continued domination of society by a wealthy white patriarchy. The changes in the educational and career opportunities for women, however, indicate that public attitudes have changed and probably will continue to do so. Women should be vigilant to make sure they have access to all of the organizations and institutions (educational, business, and social) that enable them to display qualities of leadership. One reason that several women have attempted to gain admission to military academies such as the Virginia Military Institute and the Citadel may be the perception that military training develops leadership qualities that are valuable for careers in business and politics.

If the male standard continues to be predominant in American political culture, the likelihood that women will ever attain positions of leadership in proportion to their numbers is uncertain. Women will always start off at a disadvantage when competing with men, and they will have to win in spite of their gender. Society's consciousness regarding the diversity of attitudes toward leadership in society needs to be raised, and indeed it can be raised as society learns more about the leadership exercised by women in organizations and social movements. Women are still unrepresented at the top levels of major corporations; however, many have become successful entrepreneurs, managing their own small- and medium-sized businesses. Women's success in the political arena and the continued entry of women into the political elite are fundamental to changes in society's attitude toward leadership and in women's perception of their own abilities as political leaders. Women who have attained positions of leadership and responsibility in political organizations and institutions are role models for others, demonstrating (to society as well) the leadership skills that women have to offer.

WOMEN'S POLITICAL PARTICIPATION: A CLOSER LOOK

Women's success in gaining formal access to the halls of power is a relatively recent phenomenon, but women have been active in the pursuit of diverse social policy objectives for more than two centuries. Feminist scholars such as Glenna Matthews have only recently begun to document the important role that women have played in shaping public policy.[6] These works provide a clearer picture of American society, past and present. They extoll women's contributions and thus encourage women to participate more actively at higher levels of political organizations and governmental institutions. In this section we explore the history of what Matthews calls "the rise of public woman."

Women's Political Involvement, 1840–1970

As mentioned earlier, women were active in attempting to influence the policy process even before they gained the right to vote. Why, then, has the image of the apolitical woman prevailed? The responsibility must lie at least partly within the discipline of political science. Influenced by traditional notions of appropriate sex-role behavior, many scholars fostered a perception of politics as a "man's game." They did not think of women's involvement in reform movements as being political; rather, they argued that women's interest in child care, health, and education followed naturally from their role as nurturer and that women's involvement in causes such as prohibition and abolition were appropriate for them as guardians of the nation's morality.

Feminist scholars have challenged this perception and have argued that women's involvement in these activities constituted political participation. They point out that even before the Civil War, when women were excluded from voting and holding public office, they spoke out publicly against slavery and participated in the activities of the Underground Railroad. Women were involved in educating the children of slaves, an action that violated many state laws at the time and one that could have serious political consequences. Women were also part of the union movement in the United States in the 1840s. As the nation became more industrialized, there arose a need for groups that would give voice to workers' concerns; women played key roles in early attempts to achieve humane conditions in American factories.

The securing of the right to vote was indeed the key to the beginning of the political empowerment of women. According to Glenna Matthews, the successes of the women's suffrage movement affected women's subsequent efforts in two ways. First, the parades and protests staged by the suffrage movement made many women realize the value of utilizing ritualized public behavior in the pursuit of women's interests. Such demonstrations proved to women that rather than relying on sympathetic men to advance women's causes and interests (as Abigail Adams did when she asked John to "remember the ladies") they could act for themselves. Second, women recognized that intense politicking of officeholders and important members of political parties was a valuable tactic in the pursuit of women's interests. Matthews observes that nineteenth century middle-class women were expected to be high-minded and to maintain decorum, but

> following the failure of the Reconstruction Amendments to enfranchise women, [Elizabeth Cady] Stanton and [Susan B.] Anthony had begun to push in a somewhat different direction, willing to anger their opponents, for example, as they demanded justice for women. Under [Carrie

Chapman] Catt's tutelage, women began to operate in a fashion that was forceful without being confrontational. . . . Catt personally lobbied Woodrow Wilson, asking him for advice and trying to associate him with the cause. If this approach surrendered some of the moral high ground women had been able to stake out, it may have ensured the victories of these years.[7]

After passage of the Nineteenth Amendment, women began to participate in political parties, but they often found their most important allies outside the mainstream of American politics. Women's political "friends" were most likely to be fellow reformers or those who took an even more radical perspective. The Socialist Party, for example, supported women's suffrage, as did other groups involved in the Progressive movement. The question of whether to ally with mainstream political forces led to theoretical, strategic, and tactical debates within the women's movement, which in some instances led to serious divisions. Moreover, the winner-take-all and single-member district aspects of the electoral system discouraged women from creating their own political party.

Women's political activity in the 1920s and 1930s was thus limited to lobbying political parties at the local level and participating in a wide variety of reform movements; women also held meetings and attended trials. But many of the hoped-for gains in terms of access to educational opportunity and to economic and political power never really materialized. Instead, women often wound up in a separate sphere of women's bureaus, auxiliaries, and occupations. As Matthews puts it, "women who thought they were establishing a beachhead in male-dominated institutions most often found themselves in some form of female ghetto."[8] This form of ghettoization plagued women until the beginnings of the modern feminist movement in the 1960s and the attendant changes in the lives of women—part of the cultural change discussed in Chapter 2. Women continued to participate in a range of civic organizations, but they became more involved in partisan political activity (though still performing the menial tasks in political campaigns) and in the effort to influence public policies.

In the 1970s, as Mayor Landrieu made clear, partisan politics was considered a "man's game," and civic movements were regarded as not part of politics. Since the 1970s, however, the gender gap in partisan political activity has been narrowing. Women's perceptions of the value of such activity have been influenced by implementation of public policies such as Title IX of the Education Act of 1972 (which prohibits discrimination on the basis of sex in admissions to all graduate and professional schools that receive federal funding), the battle for passage of the Equal Rights Amendment, the increase in women's employment outside the home, debate over the abortion issue, the rise of groups such as the National Women's Political Caucus, and the opinions voiced by women role models. But why do some women choose to participate whereas others do not? How are women who participate different from those who do not? Were they provided different opportunities? These questions are addressed in the next section.

Types of Political Women

In the late 1970s, Rita Mae Kelly and Mary Boutilier described three categories of political women: the private woman, the public woman, and the achieving woman. These ideal types were based on three dimensions related to the socialization process. The first dimension was the difference in sex-role concept between the traditional, passive woman and the modern, activist woman. The second dimension was the woman's extent of control over her life space. The third dimension was political saliency, that is, the extent to which politics and political activity were relevant to the woman's life space.[9] Kelly and Boutilier argued that the most important prerequisite for the development of political behavior by women was a moderately activist (modern) sex-role concept. A woman who adhered to the traditional, passive sex-role concept, which prevented her from having much control over her life space, was identified as the private woman. Acceptance of the passive role prevented her from behaving in nontraditional ways and encouraged her to participate only at the minimum level of civic obligation, such as voting. This type of woman tended to see politics as reflecting the cultural norms of a male-dominated socioeconomic and political structure. Kelly and Boutilier explained that politics was of little importance to this woman's life space because it had a minimal impact upon her primary area of concern—the family. As a result, she was unlikely to do anything more than vote. The second type, the public woman, generally had a moderately activist sex-role concept, so she exhibited many types of political behavior, depending on the amount of control she had over her life space and the saliency of her political experiences. She saw political participation as more than just civic obligation; it was reward and punishment salient as well as a mechanism for achieving her own goals. The public woman was likely to engage in partisan and nonpartisan volunteer activities such as organizing registration drives and organizing and participating in political campaigns focusing on specific issues. Her participation was often on a part-time basis or in a supportive role, depending on her responsibilities as a wife and mother; her activities were constrained by the demands of her husband's career, his attitudes, and his connections. The third type, the achieving woman, attained fame in the political sphere either by election to public office or by being part of a revolutionary group that opposed the existing political regime. She had a strong sense of personal political effectiveness, a high degree of control over her life space, and a strongly activist sex-role concept. The achieving woman ignored cultural norms about the traditional role of women in society, became a political actor, and effectively utilized political channels to achieve social and political change.

In sum, women who participated more actively in politics had three things in common: an attitudinal frame of reference that did not accept the traditional view of a woman's proper role in society; opportunities for political participation; and a sense that political activity was something more than civic duty. Women who became members of the political elite changed the nature of political participation, not only for themselves but for all women.

There have been substantial changes in the political participation of women since 1978, when Kelly and Boutilier created their categories of political women. Indeed, in the presidential election of 1996, which has been called the "Year of the Soccer Mom," women constituted one of the key electoral swing constituencies. A particular type of woman—concerned about family finances, the well-being of her parents, and the future of her children—was viewed as the key to victory. Since the late 1970s, women have entered the work force in greater numbers to maintain or increase family income, have become increasingly involved in the care of aging parents, and have become aware that a whole range of external forces that may be difficult for them to control (television violence, street gangs, and crime) have an adverse impact on their children. The "private woman" of Kelly and Boutilier now sees government as important to her family's well-being. Public policy issues such as a 15 percent tax cut, V-chips for television sets, loans for higher education, school uniforms, access to abortion, and the future of Social Security are now part of her world. At the same time, there are now many women role models in a variety of fields—television reporters and news anchors, bank officials, legislators, and Supreme Court justices. As educational, economic, and political opportunities increase, the culture becomes more accepting of women in these roles, and therefore the transition to "achieving woman" status becomes easier for each successive generation of women.

Breaking Down the Barriers to Political Participation

In view of today's increasingly complex problems, it would not be reasonable to deny a large segment of the population the opportunity to participate in policy making, as women were in the past. Not only would those individuals lose by not having their opinions heard, but society would lose by not being able to take advantage of their intelligence, skills, talents, and perspectives. Yet despite all the compelling arguments in favor of increasing the participation of women in the political process, women are still underrepresented among the political elite. Table 6-1 shows that the percentage of women in elective office has at least doubled since 1975. However, the percentages are still low, given that women constitute more than one-half of the population. The underrepresentation of women among the political elite appears to stem from two interrelated sets of problems—environmental/structural and attitudinal—that have created barriers to women's political participation, including sexual discrimination. Environmental/structural barriers include (1) the family responsibilities placed on women by society (sociocultural); (2) the limited career opportunities available to women (economic); and (3) the American electoral and party systems (political). Attitudinal barriers include (1) attitudes of the general public concerning women's political participation; (2) attitudes of the "political gatekeepers" (party leaders) who largely control the political process; and (3) attitudes of women themselves toward political participation. The two sets of problems are interactive. The sociocultural, economic, and political barriers erected in the path of women who would be political actors have in the past hindered the development of attitudes favorable to women's elite participation. The absence of women from the traditional political elite and the consequent lack of women role models (aside from those who were active in the turn-of-the-century social movements, which were not considered political) meant that the general public did not view women as possessing the qualities necessary to be political leaders, and those who controlled access to the party machinery and party nominations had difficulty in adapting to the thought of having women in the political elite.[10]

Robert Darcy, Susan Welch, and Janet Clark have described what they call the "eligibility pool"—an intangible group of potential political candidates judged on the basis of educational status, occupational status, per-

TABLE 6-1
Women in Elective Office, 1975–1996 (percent)

Office	1975	1977	1979	1981	1983	1985	1987	1989	1991	1993	1995	1996
Congress	4	4	3	4	4	5	5	5	6	10	10	12[a]
Statewide elective	10	10	11	11	11	14	14	14	18	22	26	25
State legislatures	8	9	10	12	13	15	16	17	18	21	21	21
Mayors and municipal councils	4	8	10	10	—	14	—	—	—	—	—	—

Source: Center for the American Woman and Politics, fact sheet, Women in Elective Office 1996.

[a] Includes 1996 election.

sonal contacts, and political ties.[11] Historically, women have had difficulty gaining admission to this group, and thus securing elite-level political positions, because they were denied access to many of the educational institutions that would offer them the appropriate majors or programs; thus they could not prepare for the careers that would allow them to develop personal and political contacts. Many women either did not view active political participation as desirable or consider themselves capable of elite participation. Some were inhibited from entering the political race and did not even seek their party's nomination in the primaries. Many women believed that running for and serving in an elective office were not particularly appropriate roles for a woman. They had to deal with their own concern about the public's perception that they would be "abandoning their families"; consequently, many women entered political life only after their children had grown.[12] While women stayed at home and cared for children, men, not being constrained by the same societal expectations, were developing contacts and gaining general political know-how; thus they had a competitive advantage. Moreover, traditional women's occupations such as teacher and nurse were not occupations in which women would likely be introduced to politically active individuals. By contrast, men were likely to pursue careers in business or law, which are generally considered to be training grounds for prospective political candidates. The exclusion of women from decision making and party leadership positions by the male-dominated political organizations meant that they were further denied the opportunity to develop the political skills and contacts necessary to be strong potential candidates. They were thus unlikely to seek public office for they assumed the deck was stacked against them.

Some studies have suggested that the major parties have seemed reluctant to nominate women candidates.[13] McGlen and O'Connor have argued that there appeared to be a "hidden quota" as to the number of women that both the politicians and the public were willing to accept, although some positions at various levels of government were designated as "women's positions" (in much the same way that some state political parties used to balance party tickets ethnically) and most often they were not executive positions.[14] But should responsibility for these discriminatory attitudes lie with party leaders or with the general public? Did party leaders believe that women were incapable of leading and making decisions? Or did they discourage women's candidacies because they feared that the voting public would reject women candidates as being incapable? Since a primary goal of the political party is to get its candidates elected to office, and since candidates have become increasingly dependent upon organizational campaign support (including financial contributions), party officials were reluctant to nominate women for fear that they would not be able to gain the type of support necessary to win. Women candidates thus found themselves in an ironic position: unable to attract large organizational contributions because organizations did not think women could win, they lost because they could not successfully run a modern political campaign. Some women have inherited public positions on the death of their spouse, but they have usually been viewed only as caretakers who would finish out the spouse's term, although a few did win subsequent elections in their own right. Women are now committing themselves to political elite activity earlier (that is, not waiting until their children have grown) and are attempting to develop politically relevant careers and skills. Women's groups are now practicing "pipeline politics," helping women achieve success at lower levels and attempting to ensure that it translates into success at higher levels. (Senator Barbara Mikulski of Maryland, who worked her way up from a position in the Baltimore city government, identified herself after her 1986 victory as a "twenty year overnight success story."[15])

The success of women in the elections of 1992 (which has been called "The Year of the Woman") demonstrated that attitudinal barriers are beginning to fall. But the results of the off-year elections of 1994 (dubbed by some the "Year of the Angry White Male") raised a significant question about whether the earlier gains made by women were an aberration or a harbinger. The results of the 1996 elections appeared to send a mixed message for women. Record numbers of women ran for office. The number of women candidates for Congress increased, but only slightly. Female incumbents were reelected overwhelmingly (as were male incumbents). Female challengers won some competitive races, but many were soundly defeated in noncompetitive districts (as were male challengers). At the congressional level, 238 women sought the nomination of one of the two major parties (12 Democrats and 10 Republicans for the Senate, and 136 Democrats and 80 Republicans for the House of Representatives) and 130 actually ran in the November elections (5 Democrats and 4 Republicans for the Senate, and 77 Democrats and 44 Republicans for the House). Of these candidates, 2 women won in the Senate (1 Democrat and 1 Republican) and 50 won in the House (35 Democrats and 15 Republicans). In the 1996 gubernatorial races, 9 women filed (4 Democrats and 5 Republicans), 6 won their primaries (3 Democrats and 3 Republicans), but only 1 candidate won (Jeanne Shaheen, Democrat from New Hampshire).[16] As a proportion of all available positions in the two major parties, women thus constituted 14 percent of all candidates for the House of Representatives, 13 percent of all Senate candidates, and 27 percent of all gubernatorial candidates. Since women have been estimated to constitute 52 percent of the voters in the 1996 elections, they are still woefully underrepresented among the nominees of the major parties for gubernatorial and congressional positions.

Perhaps of greatest concern to women have been signs that voters in some states are willing to ban affirmative action policies that have given preference to women and minorities in state hiring, contracting, and college admissions since the 1970s. The passage of legislation similar to California's Proposition 209 (the California Civil Rights Initiative), which was approved by 54 percent of the voters in November 1996 and upheld by the United States Court of Appeals for the Ninth Circuit on April 8, 1997 (thus overturning an injunction issued by a federal district judge blocking its implementation), could undermine many of women's gains in these areas.

For many women, making the leap from observer to active participant in the political process has been facilitated by women's organizations and women officeholders. Women's organizations, which include feminist organizations such as the National Organization for Women, the National Women's Political Caucus, and the Women's Campaign Fund, actively encourage women to seek political office and provide them with valuable campaign support, including financial assistance. Women who are actively involved in such organizations also benefit from the opportunity to develop leadership skills. Susan J. Carroll and Wendy S. Strimling studied the attitudes of women who held elective positions at various levels of government. These women reported that they had found women's organizations (in particular, the National Women's Political Caucus, the National Organization for Women, and the League of Women Voters) to be especially important in encouraging them to seek public office and actively supportive of their candidacies. Approximately one-half of the women legislators and one-quarter of the county commissioners surveyed belonged to feminist organizations, and about one-half of the women legislators either were or had been members of the League of Women Voters. As previously mentioned, women receive little support (financial or otherwise) from other political organizations, so the support of women's groups is particularly important, Carroll and Strimling suggest, for women attempting to become active in party organizations.[17]

As both supporters and mentors, women officeholders have drawn increasing numbers of women into political activity. Carroll and Strimling point out that many women in elective office said they gained valuable political experience and skills at the side of other women officeholders— serving either as their legislative or administrative aides or as aides on their campaign staffs when they were seeking elective office. To the extent that women who got their political start in this manner provide the same assistance to other women, they establish an alternative entry point to politics, outside the traditionally male-dominated organizations, and thus help to increase the number of women in politics.

Incumbency has in the past limited the opportunity of women (and men) to compete for positions that they would otherwise have a realistic chance of winning. Although it has been less of a barrier in recent years, with the increase in negative public attitudes toward government and politicians in general, incumbency is still an especially difficult problem for women to overcome because of their traditional lack of access to party nominations. Incumbents have always had extraordinary advantages such as name recognition, party support, and generous campaign funding that few challengers could overcome. Incumbents are, of course, very difficult to dislodge in the many congressional districts that are relatively noncompetitive. Senators and representatives who have seniority also have increased institutional power that can be translated into benefits for their constituents, frequently resulting in increased interest group and popular support for those who show they can "deliver for the district."

Some research has suggested that women have been about as successful in elections as men when party and incumbency of the opposing candidate are controlled for. A 1994 study by the National Women's Political Caucus found that men and women major-party candidates who ran in general elections for Congress or for governor between 1972 and 1992 and for seats in state legislatures from 1986 to 1992 were equally likely to be successful. Female incumbents were just as likely to win reelection (96 percent) as were male incumbents (95 percent). Women running for open seats (those to which no incumbent is seeking reelection) won almost as much of the time (48 percent) as did men. Women challengers to incumbents were almost as likely to win (4 percent) as were men (6 percent).[18] Even in the 1992 elections, when there was a larger number of open seats and more women than ever before ran for office, the electoral success rates did not vary. According to the National Women's Political Caucus study, if half of the challengers and half of the open-seat candidates were women, they would hold one-third of the seats by the year 2000.

The reason why there are still so many more men than women in elite political positions is perhaps not that women have been less successful candidates but rather that they have not run. Nearly two-thirds of the one thousand likely voters who were the subjects of a National Women's Political Caucus poll said they think women have a tougher time winning elections than men. Caucus director Jody Newman, author of the study, suggests that this perception may contribute to women's reluctance to run for office.[19] The perception will change, of course, if more women win elections for political office.

Passage of the term limits proposal could create more opportunities for women to run, but it could have a deleterious effect as well. Moreover, a continuation of negative public attitudes toward government and politicians in general could either help or hinder women candidates. Anti-incumbent feelings benefited women in the 1992 and 1994 elections but did not appear to have an impact in the elections of 1996. Eventually women incumbents may be perceived not as the "outsiders" described by Barbara Boxer but as part of the "insider establishment." However, female incumbents and challengers can argue that the perspective they bring to policy problems and the solutions they propose are different from those of male incumbents and thus do not have an insider orientation. Women do not have to worry just yet about being called insiders. The percentage of women in the ranks of the political elite is still nowhere near the percentage of women in the general population or the percentage of women who vote. But just how many women are part of the political elite?

WOMEN AS OFFICEHOLDERS

The increase in women's political consciousness and in opportunities for their meaningful participation would lead us to expect that women will become increasingly visible as political actors. Although the number of women who participate in politics continues to increase, the percentage of women who hold legislative, executive, and judicial positions at the national and state levels is still relatively small.[20] The number of women in elective positions increased significantly as a result of the 1992 elections. The increase in the number of women in judicial positions and in appointed administrative positions has largely been the result of women's increased access to legal education and professional opportunities. Women now have available to them a path to the political elite that was formerly reserved for men. As previously mentioned, women who attain elite positions can serve as mentors for the women members of their staffs and appoint women to positions of political power, thus further increasing the opportunities available to women.

Although appointments of women at the national level capture most of the public attention, gains for women have been greatest at the state and local levels. It is at these levels that most people become interested in investing their time and energy to correct a wide range of problems. Local issues such as crime, the quality of education, potential environmental hazards, and cleaner streets are what initially spur many people to take political action. The story of Carolyn McCarthy is an example (see Chapter 7). Many citizens feel that their ability to influence national issues is limited by such factors as access, time, connections, and money. This is generally not the case at the local level, for people are more likely to have a good understanding of the dynamics of a local problem and to know where to go to have it addressed, as well as who the key players are in influencing a decision. In the not-too-distant past, local politics was, for many women, the only avenue to which they had access. For many women today, it is still the most accessible. Moreover, the local level is where many of the problems that are of most concern to women are addressed, and consequently where many women are introduced to political gladiatorial combat.

In many respects, the community activities in which many women participate enable them to gain useful training for their political careers, for they often meet like-minded women activists who have experience in organizing at the grass-roots level. At the same time, these types of political participation may reinforce in women an approach to politics that is distinct from that of men, influencing not only the issues they pursue but the interactive behaviors they exhibit (deemphasizing partisanship and emphasizing cooperation to achieve common objectives) once they are elected or appointed to governmental positions.

More women have become political actors, and women have become more visible political actors. Barbara Jordan was at one time viewed as a political oddity. In contrast, women have now been appointed to the Supreme Court and to high-level cabinet positions; they have received their party's vice-presidential nomination and have been elected to Congress. Women are now mayors of big cities, state governors, and campaign managers of national candidates. The number of women referenced on the front pages of newspapers, the proportion of front-page photographs featuring women, and the number of women interviewed as news sources have all increased.[21] Women now view elite political positions as attainable; they are aware that they now have a broad range of opportunities to pursue a political career and organizations that support them. (We might still occasionally be reminded that not all people like this relatively new situation, however.)

Women owe a debt of gratitude to women like Elizabeth Cady Stanton, Lucretia Mott, and Susan B. Anthony. Their energy and commitment in demanding and achieving suffrage for women inspired the leaders of the modern women's movement and ultimately changed American political culture. They were role models who encouraged women to persevere and to organize in support of women's rights and women's issues. Today's role models are actors on the American political stage. Their progress may similarly inspire other women (perhaps the granddaughter or great granddaughter of Eleanora Tomec) to enter a political race; one of them may be the first woman president.

The remainder of this chapter focuses on women in the judicial system, women in the legislatures, and women in state and local government and the different avenues they have pursued in achieving their success.

The Judicial System

It is in the judicial system (at all levels—local, state, and national) that women have made their largest gains and where the impact of cultural change can be most clearly observed. At the national level, the most well-known success stories are those of Supreme Court Justices Sandra Day O'Connor and Ruth Bader Ginsburg and Attorney General Janet Reno, who were appointed to their positions by both Democratic and Republican presidents. At the local and state levels, women have worked their way up to positions of power and authority in prosecutors' offices, in local courts, and in the state attorney's office. All of this has taken place in a legal and judicial system that until recently was dominated by men.

The fundamental factor that accounts for the increased numbers of women officeholders in the judicial system is their access to a legal education. With the passage of Title IX of the Education Act of 1972, the doors to a legal education were opened wide and the number of women in law schools has increased tenfold.[22] But as Earlean McCarrick points out, "More than the passage of time and an increasing number of women lawyers are necessary for women to achieve positions of power in proportion to their numbers. . . . That will require greater receptivity to women on the part of the 'opportunity structure'—those who participate in selecting judges and in securing for young law students and lawyers those positions which put them in line for selection as judges."[23] Jimmy Carter was the first U.S. president to open up the judicial system for women. Although he did not have the opportunity during his one term to appoint the first woman to the Supreme Court, he substantially increased the number of women appointees to federal courts, district courts, and appeals courts. Relatively fewer women were appointed during the presidencies of Ronald Reagan and George Bush; however, Reagan was the first president to appoint a woman (Sandra Day O'Connor) to the Supreme Court. With the election of Bill Clinton in 1992 and 1996 and his emphasis on having a government that reflects the diversity of society, women have gained another seat on the Supreme Court (Ruth Bader Ginsburg) and two cabinet positions (Janet Reno as attorney general and Madeleine Albright as secretary of state). Since 1993, more than 55 percent of Clinton's appointees have been women and members of ethnic minorities, compared with 14 percent in the Reagan administration and 26 percent in the Bush administration. Sheldon Goldman, professor of political science at the University of Massachusetts, views these appointees as "well-qualified, competent people." Indeed, 67 percent of Clinton's judicial nominees have received the highest possible rating from the nonpartisan American Bar Association—a higher percentage than received by the nominees of any other president. The Clinton appointees are also viewed as being less ideological than those of the Reagan and Bush administrations, who, according to Goldman, "dominate the judiciary today."[24] In his second term, Clinton may have the opportunity to replace one or two Supreme Court justices, and perhaps the Court will move toward positions more supportive of women's issues. There is even speculation that if Chief Justice William H. Rehnquist retires, Ginsburg may replace him, thus becoming the first woman to have such an honor. Clearly, a president who seeks to increase women's opportunities can have a substantial impact on women's ultimate success in attaining relative parity in the political arena.

When women in the judicial system have had the opportunity to perform, they have usually met with favorable responses by their peers and the general public. Marcia Clark, one of the lead prosecutors in the O. J. Simpson trial, was generally applauded for her legal skills (even though some observers appeared to be more interested in her hairstyle and her ability to balance her public and private lives). Some critics initially argued that Janet Reno's appointment was intended to meet a quota rather than to fill a position (especially after the withdrawals of Kimba Wood and Zoë Baird), but for the most part she has drawn praise for her decisiveness and her willingness to accept responsibility for her decisions in such actions as the Branch Davidian crisis in Waco, the "Travelgate" problems of the Clinton administration, and the firing of FBI Director William Sessions.

The judicial system is a key arena where issues of importance to women (such as spousal abuse, date rape, nonpayment of child support, and access to health care services) are decided on a regular basis, and thus one where women can exert significant influence. Nancy McGlen and Karen O'Connor have analyzed the impact of Sandra Day O'Connor's appointment to the Supreme Court. Although she was appointed by Republican president Ronald Reagan and is generally considered to be part of the Court's conservative bloc, Justice O'Connor has supported the positions of women's rights advocates in 66 percent of the sexual discrimination cases decided by the Court. She also wrote the majority opinion reaffirming a woman's right to have an abortion when the decision in *Roe v. Wade* (1973) was challenged in *Planned Parenthood of Southeastern Pennsylvania v. Casey* (1992).[25]

The Legislatures

Although women still hold a relatively small percentage of the positions in Congress and the state legislatures, and achieved only moderate gains in the 1994 and 1996 elections, they clearly have begun the transition from political oddity to legislative force. (Legislation proposed by women in the 104th Congress that is of concern to women is discussed in Chapter 7; see the box on pages 144 and 145.) The increase in the number of women in Congress since 1967 is shown in Figure 6-1. In the 90th Congress (1967–1968) there were 11 women (6 Democrats and 5 Republicans), compared with 52 women (36 Democrats, 16 Republicans) in the 105th Congress (1997–1998)—a 500 percent increase. In the Senate (Figure 6-2), the number of women remained fairly constant but increased substantially beginning with the 102d Congress (1991–1992). The Senate figures for the 104th and 105th Congresses remain high because senators are elected for six-year terms. The off-year congressional elections could indicate whether the trend in women's representation will continue. (Will the women who won in 1992 be reelected in 1998, and will more women capture Senate seats?) In the House of Representatives (Figure 6-3), the number of women increased gradually, but there was a large increase

FIGURE 6-1

Number of Women in Congress (90th to 105th Congresses)

Number of Women

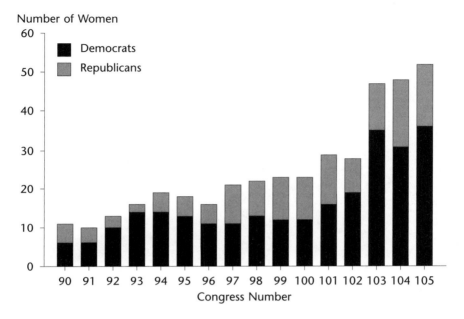

Source: Center for the American Woman and Politics, fact sheet, *Women in Elective Office 1996.*

beginning with the 103d Congress (1993–1994). Since 1969, there has also been a steady increase in the percentage of women in the state legislatures, as shown in Figure 6-4. The percentages of women in the state legislatures in 1996 are given in descending order in Table 6-2. Table 6-1 shows the percentages of women in elective office at all levels of government from 1975 to 1996. Approximately 80 percent of the states have higher percentages of women in the state legislatures than in Congress. This is quite logical since we would expect this aspect of cultural change to begin at the local and state levels. The expectation that women will increase their numbers in Congress is thus realistic, given the increasing number of women entering politics at the local and state levels. Interestingly, as shown in Table 6-2, seven of the ten states with the smallest percentages of women in the state legislature in 1996 are located in the South, and six of the ten states with the highest percentages of women in the state legislature are Western states. Some research suggests that state legislatures with significant numbers of women operate differently than do

FIGURE 6-2
Number of Women in the Senate (90th to 105th Congresses)

Number of Women

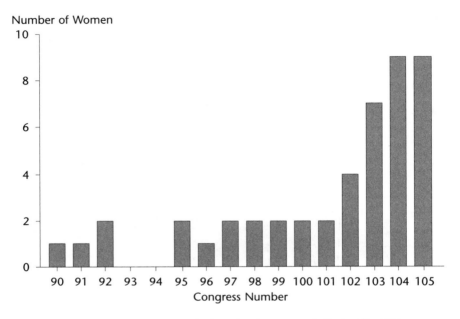

Source: Center for the American Woman and Politics, fact sheet, *Women in Elective Office 1996.*

those with small numbers of women, but the evidence thus far is inconclusive.[26]

Legislatures have traditionally been the preserve of males and have operated largely as de facto men's social clubs. It can be argued that the successful functioning of the legislative process in a pluralistic society is dependent upon bargaining, accommodation, and compromise, which are facilitated by an atmosphere of amiability and collegiality. Women in this social club environment are likely to feel like outsiders or strangers (as did Barbara Boxer). It can also be questioned whether a policy-making body that is not entirely representative of the population can produce policies that reflect a wide range of perspectives. Although the number of women in Congress is still relatively small, a woman's perspective needs to be brought to some of the issues and policies with which legislators must deal. (Boxer and her colleagues went to the Senate Democratic caucus with a point of view they believed the male legislators needed to hear.)

FIGURE 6-3

Number of Women in the House of Representatives (90th to 105th Congresses)

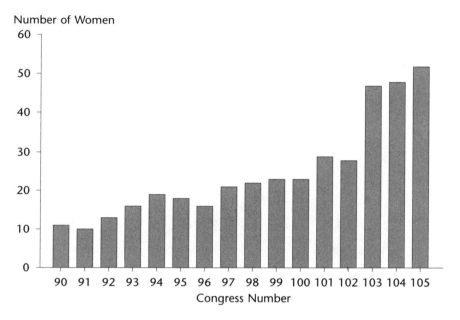

Source: Center for the American Woman and Politics, fact sheet, *Women in Elective Office 1996.*

Since the 1970s, when women began to win legislative elections, some interesting research has been done on changes in the sociodemographic characteristics of women legislators and the types of legislative positions (committee and leadership) they have attained. There has also been some analysis of the impact that the increase in the number of women has had, and possibly will have, on the operation and policies of legislative institutions.[27]

Irwin N. Gertzog has explored some of the changes that have occurred in the sociodemographic makeup of Congress: a significant decrease in the number of women who succeed to the positions of their deceased husbands, a significant increase in the number of married women, a decrease in the number of women from political families or wealthy families, an increase in the number of women who are lawyers, and an increase in the number of women who have held prior elective positions.[28] In the 1920s, a woman was considered only a temporary replacement for her deceased husband while the party decided which man would take over the seat in the

FIGURE 6-4
Percentage of Women in State Legislatures, 1969–1995

Percentage of Women

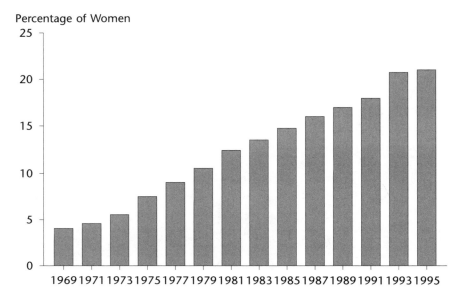

Source: Center for the American Woman and Politics, fact sheet, *Women in Elective Office 1996.*

next election; however, today she is likely to actively seek the office after having had a successful political career at other levels (state and local) or in other branches (executive and judicial). Gertzog identifies these women as "strategic politicians" and describes them as "experienced, highly motivated career public servants who carefully calculate the personal and political benefits of running for higher office, assess the probability of their winning, and determine the personal and political costs of defeat before deciding to risk the positions they hold to secure a more valued office."[29] Women who attain congressional positions are thus influenced by the changing political culture and the increasing opportunities available to them.

Gertzog analyzes the gender role orientations (gentlewoman, neutral, and feminist) and legislative role orientations (amateur, professional, and colleague) of women in Congress and develops three basic role orientations: the gentlewoman amateur, the neutral professional, and the feminist colleague. A woman member of Congress may fit any of these three categories at any time, but there is generally a historical pattern that is related to the number of women in the legislature. The gentlewoman amateur tends to be

TABLE 6-2

Percentage of Women in State Legislatures, 1996

State Rank	State	Women	State Rank	State	Women
1	Washington	39.5	26	New Mexico	20.5
2	Nevada	34.9	27	California	20.0
3	Colorado	33.0	28	Missouri	19.8
4	Arizona	30.0	29	Hawaii	19.7
4	Oregon	30.0	30	Florida	19.4
4	Vermont	30.0	31	South Dakota	19.0
7	New Hampshire	29.7	32	Texas	18.2
8	Maryland	28.7	33	Georgia	18.2
9	Idaho	28.6	34	New York	18.0
10	Kansas	27.9	35	Iowa	18.0
11	Connecticut	26.7	36	North Carolina	16.5
12	Maine	26.3	37	West Virginia	15.7
13	Minnesota	25.4	38	New Jersey	15.0
14	Nebraska	24.5	39	Virginia	15.0
15	Wisconsin	24.2	40	Utah	14.4
16	Massachusetts	24.0	41	North Dakota	14.3
16	Montana	24.0	42	Tennessee	13.6
16	Rhode Island	24.0	43	Arkansas	12.6
19	Ohio	23.5	44	South Carolina	12.4
20	Alaska	23.3	45	Mississippi	11.5
21	Illinois	23.2	46	Pennsylvania	11.5
22	Michigan	22.3	47	Louisiana	11.1
23	Indiana	22.0	48	Oklahoma	10.7
24	Wyoming	21.1	49	Kentucky	8.7
25	Delaware	21.0	50	Alabama	3.6

Source: Center for the American Woman and Politics, fact sheet, *Women in Elective Office 1996.*

a traditional woman who accepts the subordinate gender role and who has little interest in legislative activity or legislative experience. This category best describes the women of the 1960s and 1970s who, at most, performed some of the constituency service tasks associated with the legislative process.

The neutral professional role orientation generally refers to women who entered Congress when the number of women in Congress was still small. Many were career politicians who had succeeded in an unfriendly political culture; they were hesitant to pursue issues or agendas that would be identified as specific to women, so they generally tried to maintain as low a profile as possible while still trying to achieve their objectives. They were aware that they were being held to a different standard than were men and would be subjected to extraordinary scrutiny. This role orientation thus combines an inhibited gender role orientation with a cautionary legislative role orientation. Gertzog suggests that neutral professionals knew that "as members of a small, conspicuous minority, they would be operating within a goldfish bowl. Behavior that would be overlooked or quickly forgotten if engaged in by a male Representative would trigger derision or worse if enacted by a congresswoman. There were simply too many House members and constituents who did not need much of an excuse to interpret their activities within the framework of a female stereotype."[30] Many of these women devoted a large percentage of their time to constituency service and hoped eventually to benefit from the seniority system, which then worked to the advantage of their male colleagues. Such behavior was only a slight improvement over that of the gentlewoman amateur. According to Gertzog, neutral professionals were still opting "for the subordinate status that females have traditionally held in their relationships with males. For underlying these efforts carefully to manage their behavior and avoid calling attention to their gender was the more fundamental objective of not upsetting men. They wanted to be effective legislators, and they could not gain that reputation by 'rocking the boat'."[31] The neutral professional was thus a victim of an institution dominated by men.

The feminist colleague role orientation, which began to emerge during the 1970s, combines a feminist gender role orientation with an activist legislative role orientation. The feminist perspective of these legislators influences their legislative behavior and their analysis of public policy. They do not defer to their male colleagues and have created an organization within Congress to support women's issues (the Congressional Caucus for Women's Issues). As a result of their efforts, Congress now addresses social issues such as spousal and child abuse and sexual harassment, which have historically been thought to be outside the domain of national policy. Gertzog describes the impact that feminist colleagues have had on congressmen: "Male members' understanding of their representative responsibilities has . . . been undergoing change. Congressmen have become less likely to ignore or treat cursorily the women's constituency and they are much less diffident today about identifying with and even dramatizing their support for feminist causes."[32]

The successes of women in the legislative arena have implications for the individual women who aspire to political office, for women as a group, and for society as a whole. Sue Thomas predicts that as the proportion of women in governing bodies increases, the progress women have already made toward individual and group goals will be nearly complete. Female representatives effectively meet the needs of their constituents through service and legislative action, contribute significantly and meaningfully to policy debates, earn respect from their colleagues, and master the legislative process. As their numbers increase further, individual goals related to higher ambition will accelerate and legislative leadership will, more often, become the realm of women.[33]

Women's relatively recent success in capturing legislative seats is probably the greatest indication of the fundamental change that is occurring in the political culture. The experience of Barbara Boxer and her colleagues will likely never have to be repeated.

State and Local Governments

According to the Center for the American Woman and Politics, women held 82 (or 25.3 percent) of the 324 available statewide elective executive offices in 1996; such offices were held by women in forty-six of the fifty states. This category does not include state-level appointive positions such as those in the cabinet, on boards of trustees, or in the judicial branch; nor does it include elective positions in the judiciary, on university boards of trustees, and on state boards of education. Among the latter positions were one governor (a second governor, Jeanne Shaheen of New Hampshire, was also elected in 1996), 18 lieutenant governors, 9 attorneys general, 11 secretaries of state, 12 state treasurers, 4 state auditors, 3 state comptrollers, 11 chief state education officers, and 13 other types of state commissioner.[34]

The preeminent elective executive position in every state is that of governor. As chief executive of the state, the governor generally has a wide range of powers and responsibilities, including appointive and veto powers and budget authority; the governor plays a role in the legislative process as well. In some states, the governor is the only official (with the exception of the two senators) elected on a statewide basis, and even when the governor is one of a number of statewide elected officials, he or she is generally the focus of media attention in the state. In the late 1800s, many thought of governors as "good-time Charlies." But as Larry Sabato points out, "Once the darlings of the society pages, governors today are more concerned about the substantive work of the office than about its ceremonial aspects. . . . Once ill-prepared to govern and less prepared to lead,

governors have welcomed into their ranks a new breed of vigorous, inci-
sive, and thoroughly trained leaders."[35] Some would argue that the governorship used to be the pinnacle of the "good old boys" political network
in most states. The man who attained this position had made many friends
among party bosses and party activists, had sufficient name recognition as
a result of media attention, and had access to money—all of which enabled
him to successfully compete for the office. Virtually all these advantages
would have been denied to women. Since the 1970s, however, women
have been increasingly successful in gubernatorial races. Some of this success can be traced to changes in the nature of the governorship as described
by Sabato and to the changing opportunities for women.

As of 1996, fourteen women have been (or are) governors of their states.
The first woman to be elected governor was Nellie Taylor Ross, a
Democrat from Wyoming (the first state to enfranchise women). She was
elected to serve the two years that remained of her deceased husband's
term and was defeated in the subsequent election (1926). Miriam "Ma"
Ferguson (D-Texas; 1925–1927) and Lurleen Wallace (D-Ala.;
1966–1968) were elected as surrogates for their husbands, who could not
run for reelection. The route to the governorship for these women reflected the political culture of their times. Women were not seen as viable candidates in their own right but were viewed as substitutes or stand-ins for
their husbands. The fact that Ross and Ferguson attained the governorship
in the 1920s was somewhat remarkable.

All of the remaining woman governors won elections in their own right:
Ella Grasso (D-Conn.), Dixie Lee Ray (D-Wash.), Martha Layne Collins
(D-Ky.), Madeleine Kunin (D-Vt.), Kay Orr (R-Neb.), Rose Mofford (D-
Ariz.), Ann Richards (D-Texas), Joan Finney (D-Kan.), Barbara Roberts
(D-Ore.), Christine Todd Whitman (R-N.J.), and Jeanne Shaheen (D-
N.H.). Whitman, elected in 1994, is a popular governor who has often been
mentioned as a possible vice-presidential candidate. Shaheen is the first
woman to be elected governor of New Hampshire. The preceding list does
not suggest a geographic pattern or consistent party affiliation; most of these
governors have been Democrats, but the more recent success of Orr and
Whitman suggests that this is not a consistent trend.

The position of lieutenant governor can be a stepping-stone to the governorship, for it increases statewide exposure. In 1994, in eleven of the
forty-two states that had a lieutenant governor, that position was held by a
woman. This was a record number; interestingly, seven of the eleven lieutenant governors were Republicans.

The appointment of a woman to an administrative position can have three important consequences: First, there is the potential for a multiplier effect; women appointed to these positions are free to appoint other women to line and staff positions in administrative agencies and statewide commissions. Second, such appointments increase the likelihood that women's issues and concerns will receive higher priority on the agendas of public agencies and commissions. Third, there is the possibility of a gradual change in the culture, which begins in the public organizations to which women are appointed. Longer-term effects include changes in women's attitudes toward careers in public service and changes in the public's attitude toward women in government.

An example is the record of Ann Richards in Texas. Joanne Rajoppi argues that Richards radically changed the culture of Texas state government. Her initial cabinet-level appointments and appointments to state commissions, drawn largely from her contacts within county government and the women's movement, were intended to fulfill her campaign promise that Texas state government would no longer be the preserve of white men. Their diversity (20 percent Hispanic, 15 percent black, 46 percent female, plus several Asian and gay appointees) led Alison Cook to point out that "there is no denying that Richards' picks reflect the state's diverse population—a radical notion in Texas and one that may prove to be her most enduring legacy. Richards' appointments have also set a populist tone foreign to recent Texas politics, and agencies long cozy with the industries they police have begun to tilt citizenward."[36]

Dramatic changes have occurred in American political culture since 1920, when women gained the right to vote. The cumulative impact of the changes in gender role orientation and political attitudes, the increasing opportunities for women to participate in politics, and an attitudinal and an occupational climate more supportive of women's equality has been a change in the gender ratio of the institutions of political power. Although women are still not represented in proportion to their numbers, they have made enormous inroads into previously all-male domains. In the judicial and legal systems, in legislatures, and in state and local governments, women have begun to occupy positions in numbers significant enough to enable them to influence the cultures of these institutions, the ways they operate, and the policies they produce.

The increasing numbers of women in the political elite, although a relatively recent phenomenon, is indeed a significant one. Many scholars still question what its long-term effects will be,[37] but it is obvious that the views of Mayors Landrieu and Lindsay do not reflect today's political culture. There is perhaps no better example of cultural change than the candidate elected to the Senate in 1996 from the state of Louisiana—Mary Landrieu, Moon Landrieu's daughter.

The increased educational, economic, and political opportunities that have become available to women since the 1960s have changed women's perceptions of their abilities to win public office, as well as the public's perception of women's political viability and political acumen. After the successes of women candidates in the elections of 1992, many felt that a watershed had occurred and that women's future in politics appeared to be secure. But the outcome of the 1994 off-year elections and the criticisms leveled against some women political actors (for example, their characterization as "feminazis" by conservative talk show host Rush Limbaugh) have raised some serious questions about the future of women's role in politics. The potential roadblocks to women's continued successes are discussed in Chapter 7.

NOTES

1. Susan Tolchin and Martin Tolchin, *Clout: Womanpower and Politics* (New York: Coward, McCann and Geoghegan, 1974), 13–30.

2. Barbara Boxer with Nicole Boxer, *Strangers in the Senate: Politics and the New Revolution of Women in America* (Washington, D.C.: National Press Books, 1994), 32, 35.

3. For an expanded discussion of these ideas, see Nel Noddings, "The Gender Issue," *Educational Leadership* 49, no. 4 (December 1991–January 1992): 65–70.

4. Richard Neustadt, *Presidential Power* (New York: Wiley, 1964), 33–57.

5. Camilla Stivers, *Gender Images in Public Administration: Legitimacy and the Administrative State* (Newbury Park, Calif.: Sage Publications, 1993), 59.

6. Glenna Matthews, *The Rise of Public Woman: Woman's Power and Woman's Place in the United States, 1630–1970* (New York: Oxford University Press, 1992).

7. Ibid., 173.

8. Ibid., 177.

9. Rita Mae Kelly and Mary Boutilier, *The Making of Political Women* (Chicago: Nelson-Hall, 1978), 61–72. Although this study is based on earlier data, the three categories help to demonstrate the changes that have occurred in women's political participation.

10. Nancy E. McGlen and Karen O'Connor, *Women's Rights: The Struggle for Equality in the Nineteenth and Twentieth Centuries* (New York: Praeger, 1983), 115.

11. Robert Darcy, Susan Welch, and Janet Clark, *Women, Elections, and Representation,* 2d ed. (Lincoln: University of Nebraska Press, 1994), 105.

12. McGlen and O'Connor, *Women's Rights,* 118.

13. Ibid., 120.

14. Ibid., 121.

15. Susan M. Hartmann, *From Margin to Mainstream: American Women and Politics since 1960* (New York: Knopf, 1989), 171–173.

16. Data from Center for the American Woman and Politics, *Women Congressional and Gubernatorial Candidates 1996: Major Party Nominees—Winners and Losers as of 11/22/96* (New Brunswick, N.J.: Eagleton Institute of Politics, Rutgers University). This fact sheet is available from the Internet at http://www.rci.rutgers.edu/~cawp/cand.html.

17. Susan J. Carroll and Wendy S. Strimling, *Women's Routes to Elective Office: A Comparison with Men's* (Rutgers, N.J.: Center for the American Woman and Politics, 1983), 83–109, 136–137. It should be noted that the League of Women Voters (whose membership includes both men and women) does not support or endorse candidates (of either gender) and that women must resign as officers of the League of Women Voters if they become candidates for political office.

18. National Women's Political Caucus, "Perception and Reality: A Study Comparing the Success of Men and Women Candidates" (Washington, D.C.: National Women's Political Caucus, 1994).

19. Newman, Jody. "Perception and Reality: A Study Comparing the Success of Men and Women Candidates, Executive Summary," 1994.

20. Statistics on changes in the percentages of women officeholders are taken from fact sheets published by the Center for the American Woman and Politics: *Women in Elective Office 1994,* March 1994; *Statewide Elective Executive Women 1994,* March 1994; *Women in State Legislatures 1994,* March 1994; *Summary of Women Candidates for Selected Offices 1968–1992,* October 1994; and *Women Candidates for Governor 1970–1993,* August 1994.

21. Pippa Norris, "Through a Gendered Lens: Media Framing of International Women Leaders," 8. Paper presented at the August 1996 meeting of the American Political Science Association, San Francisco.

22. Earlean McCarrick, "Women and the Criminal Justice System," in M. Margaret Conway, David W. Ahern, and Gertrude A. Steuernagel, *Women and Public Policy: A Revolution in Progress* (Washington, D.C.: CQ Press, 1995), 172.

23. Ibid., 173.

24. "Clinton Bench Shows Diversity," *Salt Lake Tribune,* February 10, 1996.

25. Nancy E. McGlen and Karen O'Connor, *Women, Politics, and American Society* (Englewood Cliffs, N.J.: Prentice-Hall, 1995), 93.

26. For an excellent survey of the literature on this subject, see Sue Thomas, *How Women Legislate* (New York: Oxford University Press, 1994).

27. Thomas examines the backgrounds of and attitudinal and legislative differences between male and female legislators (ibid., 31–39).

28. This discussion is drawn from Chapters 2 and 3 of Irwin N. Gertzog, *Congressional Women: Their Recruitment, Integration, and Behavior,* 2d ed. (Westport, Conn.: Greenwood Press, 1995).

29. Ibid., 4.

30. Ibid., 254.

31. Ibid., 256–257.

32. Ibid., 260.

33. Thomas, *How Women Legislate,* 155.

34. Center for the American Woman and Politics, fact sheet, *Statewide Elective Executive Women 1996.*

35. Larry Sabato, *Goodbye to Good-Time Charlie: The American Governor Transformed, 1950–1975* (Washington, D.C.: CQ Press, 1983), 2.

36. Joanne Rajoppi, *Women in Office: Getting There and Staying There* (Westport, Conn.: Bergin and Garvey, 1993), 94. Ann Richards was a casualty of the Republican landslide in the 1994 off-year elections.

37. See, for example, Thomas, *How Women Legislate,* 149–158.

SUGGESTIONS FOR FURTHER READING

Boxer, Barbara, with Nicole Boxer. *Strangers in the Senate: Politics and the New Revolution of Women in America.* Washington, D.C.: National Press Books, 1994.

Carroll, Susan J. *Women as Candidates in American Politics.* 2d ed. Bloomington: Indiana University Press, 1994.

Darcy, Robert, Susan Welch, and Janet Clark. *Women, Elections, and Representation.* 2d ed. Lincoln: University of Nebraska Press, 1994.

Gertzog, Irwin N. *Congressional Women: Their Recruitment, Integration, and Behavior.* 2d ed. Westport, Conn.: Greenwood Press, 1995.

Mandel, Ruth B. *In the Running: The New Woman Candidate.* New York: Ticknor and Fields, 1981.

Matthews, Glenna. *The Rise of Public Woman: Woman's Power and Woman's Place in the United States, 1630–1970.* New York: Oxford University Press, 1992.

Phillips, Anne. *Engendering Democracy.* University Park: Pennsylvania State University Press, 1991.

Rajoppi, Joanne. *Women in Office: Getting There and Staying There.* Westport, Conn.: Bergin and Garvey, 1993.

Thomas, Sue. *How Women Legislate.* New York: Oxford University Press, 1994.

Tolchin, Susan, and Martin Tolchin. *Clout: Womanpower and Politics.* New York: Coward, McCann and Geoghegan, 1974.

Witt, Linda, Karen M. Paget, and Glenna Matthews. *Running as a Woman: Gender and Power in American Politics.* New York: Free Press, 1994.

CHAPTER 7

Women, Politics, and Cultural Change

Change is the key word to use in characterizing the differences in the lives of three generations of women—Eleanora Tomec, her daughters, and her granddaughters. It is also the key word to use in assessing the significance of the twentieth century for women, culture, and political participation. Clearly there has been a gradual redefinition of what it means to be a woman. Some women still consider home and family to be the center of their lives. For others, career concerns dominate; but life may be a juggling act—sometimes joyful, sometimes depressing, always challenging—in which they attempt to meet the needs of family members, employers, and friends. Although more opportunities are now available, not all women have the same range of options; they still may be limited by class, age, and race. Many women have the motivation and the resources to participate in some form of political activity. Those who make a greater commitment may become active in their political party and even run for office, they may become members of the political elite, or they may participate in political protests.

In the centuries that separate Abigail Adams's entreaty to her husband to "remember the ladies" and Barbara Boxer's entreaty as one of the "strangers in the Senate," women have succeeded in opening the doors to political power. Those who have become part of the political elite are now "at the table," where issues of importance to women and to the nation—in such areas as health care, education, the environment, and foreign policy—are decided. But have increased political participation and access to positions of power and responsibility made a difference in women's lives? In the quality of life of most Americans? Have changes in society and in women's attitudes and beliefs resulted in significant changes in their roles in the political arena? Has there been a change in the policy agenda or the political process? These are some of the questions addressed in this chapter.

Between the elections of 1992 and 1994 women attained legislative successes such as passage of the Family and Medical Leave Act (1993) and witnessed the appointment of the first woman to a high-level cabinet position. Women also heard some among them characterized as "feminazis" and saw Hillary Rodham Clinton attacked for her role in the Clinton administration's failed attempt to reform the health care delivery system in the United States. Was this just politics as usual? Was it merely an expected reaction to change? Or was it a reaction against women that will result in their withdrawal from some or all types of political activity? Maybe "Hillary bashing" is an expression of deeper cultural concerns about the emergence of women on the political stage. Change is scary, and perhaps none more so than the changes associated with women's increasing rates of political participation at all levels. The elections of 1996 did not provide clear signals regarding cultural changes that may affect the role of women in politics. There was a record gender gap (described by some as a "gender chasm") in voting for the Democratic and Republican candidates for president. A president who is generally considered supportive of women's issues was reelected, but so were a Republican-controlled House and Senate. A significant percentage of the congressional members who were first elected in the 1994 off-year elections, who were largely responsible for passage of the Republican "Contract with America" (some parts of which were viewed as inimical to women's interests), were returned to office. Record numbers of women ran for office, but the number who were elected and who hold positions of power is still small, given that women constitute a majority of the population. What does it all mean? In seeking answers about the future of women and politics, it may be helpful to reflect upon the past.

FROM THE PAST TO THE PRESENT

Eleanora Tomec, Barbara Jordan, Elizabeth Cady Stanton, and Barbara Boxer led very different lives at different times in history. These women also differ in terms of race, age, religion, education, employment, and marital status, so is it even possible to discuss commonalities, to view women's political participation as something that can have meaning beyond the lives of individual women? Gender both shapes and is shaped by culture, and it is commonalities of gender—what it means to be a woman who is influencing and influenced by American culture—that give legitimacy to this analysis.

In this book we have focused on the fundamental cultural changes that have occurred. Chapter 1 introduced the story of women's political participation in the United States. Although women were denied the right to vote until 1920, they had long participated in movements to bring about change. The Daughters of Liberty played a role in the American Revolution. Women were involved in the abolition movement and other movements for social justice. Although they could not vote, women were involved politically, even when they had to work outside the mainstream or were confined to roles that at the time were considered appropriate for women.

The lives of Eleanora Tomec and her daughters illustrate some of the major cultural changes that have occurred in women's lives. Eleanora was typical of her generation, for she did not graduate from college. Her daughters, typical of their generations, did. Eleanora's working life was somewhat atypical of her generation, but her profession was not. Her daughters' working lives, each different from the other, reveal the diversity of opportunities increasingly available to women—and the challenges they present. Politically, Eleanora identified with party and faith, not gender. Although she was a regular voter, she participated in few political activities. Her daughters, both of whom identify less strongly with the Democratic Party and the Catholic Church than did their mother, vote regularly and have participated in peaceful demonstrations and other forms of political activity. They are more conscious of the role gender has played in their lives; the older daughter has reentered the work force after her divorce; the younger daughter holds a nontraditional job and delayed childbearing and marriage. The choices Eleanora made about her life were based primarily on her roles as wife and mother. But her younger daughter did not delay or abandon her career plans to be a wife and mother. Instead, she had to navigate the unfamiliar waters of role change, trying somehow to be at once wife, mother, and employee.

In many respects, Eleanora's daughters had more of the autonomy and self-determination that are the foundation of a liberal culture. But they had this advantage in large part because of their mother's contribution. Eleanora recognized the value of an education, and it was her earnings from a secretarial job that financed their college educations and helped them launch their careers. Eleanora's daughters were also able to take advantage of the opportunities that began to open up for women—opportunities not available to Eleanora.

Eleanora's sacrifice has indirectly increased the opportunities of her granddaughters as well. Eleanora's older granddaughter is a college student majoring in science—a field traditionally dominated by men. Material things mean little to her, and she remains open to new experiences. Eleanora's younger granddaughter, a nursing major, wants to help people but also to make money. Aware of the financial difficulties caused by her parents' divorce, she wants to be certain that when she marries, her financial future will be in her own hands.

Eleanora's personal decisions and political choices have had an impact, direct or indirect, on the lives of her daughters and granddaughters. They are also part of the larger impact women have had on American culture and politics. Political participation for Eleanora meant primarily carrying out her civic duty by voting; for her daughters and granddaughters it means much more.

Cultural change influences how women acquire notions of gender-appropriate behavior, and these notions affect their political participation (Chapter 2). Political socialization includes both direct and indirect political learning. The major agents of political socialization are family, school, and workplace, along with situational and structural factors. Gender and race can shape political beliefs and ambitions, as they did Barbara Jordan's. Three key concepts in the discussion of political socialization are acculturation, the social clock, and gender consciousness.

Acculturation, a term usually used to describe immigrants' adaptation to a new culture, is also used in the context of the historical foreignness of politics to women. Politics, which has traditionally been a male domain with a language dominated by metaphors of power, has been changed by the entry of women. The social clock refers to society's expectations concerning behavior that is appropriate at various stages of life. The lives of Barbara Jordan and of Eleanora Tomec and her daughters can be analyzed in this light. Women's political participation has been influenced by their gender consciousness—that is, how women define themselves as women.

Gender differences have been found in political attitudes and policy preferences (Chapter 3). Possible explanations for the existence of gender differences in political orientation include gender role socialization and the differential treatment of men and women on the basis of differences in educational attainment, occupation, and income. Data from public opinion surveys, such as the American National Election Studies, reveal some specific gender differences in public policy preferences on issues such as support for expansion or contraction of government programs and services, support for the use of force to solve problems, abortion policy, affirmative action, sexual harassment, and trustworthiness and effectiveness of the federal government. Men and women have also been found to differ in their knowledge about government and politics, their party identification, and their candidate preferences.

Women's group consciousness has been found to influence their political orientation and policy preferences (Chapter 4). Women have been categorized as feminists, potential feminists, and nonfeminists. Feminist orientation can affect political attitudes concerning a number of issues, such as federal spending for child care and public education, abortion policy, and sexual harassment. Feminists tend to be more supportive than potential feminists or nonfeminists of these two spending programs, but there seems to be no significant difference among the three groups in support for federal funding for crime prevention and aid to the poor, or for financial aid to college students. These findings suggest the need to pay attention to differences in political orientation, both among women and between men and women.

Women's political participation can be analyzed in terms of their involvement in various forms of political activity, turnout of women voters, and their voting patterns (Chapter 5). A number of trends emerge, reflecting the impact of employment and educational status on women's political participation. For example, women with different levels of education have different policy concerns. American National Election Studies data on presidential elections from 1952 to 1992 are the basis for a comparison of men's and women's participation in five types of political activities: working for a candidate or political party, contributing money, attending a political meeting or campaign rally, trying to persuade someone else to vote, and wearing a campaign button or displaying a campaign sticker. People sometimes participate in politics when asked to do so. Men are more likely than women to make campaign contributions. But men are also more likely than women to be asked to make such contributions. Research indicates that women are less likely than men to participate politically. Women are more likely than men to vote, yet their rates of participation in other forms of political activity lag behind those of men. It is necessary to look beyond traditional forms of political participation, such as voting and campaigning, to find examples of women's political involvement, however. Women are frequently involved in community activities that, although not directly political, have political consequences. These activities enable them to acquire leadership skills that are useful in more traditional political activities. Theoretically, those who have the resources to participate are more likely to do so. The changes that have occurred in women's lives in the areas of education and employment are increasing their resources, which may be linked to increasing levels of political participation.

Women who develop feminist consciousness are more likely to become involved in some form of political activity. The evidence presented in Chapter 4 suggests that younger women, women who are better educated, and women who are employed are more likely to display feminist consciousness. Given women's increasing levels of education and participation in the work force, the possibility exists that feminist consciousness will also increase, and along with it, women's political participation.

As the political culture has changed, and as women's lives have changed, more women have become members of the political elite (Chapter 6). Although women continue to be underrepresented, they are making progress in joining what previously has been a male domain. Historically, women have had an impact on public policy even though they were denied entry into the political elite. Now that there are fewer attitudinal and structural barriers to their membership, women will likely have a greater impact on public policy.

A male standard has dominated American politics. Qualities traditionally associated with men, such as decisiveness and aggressiveness, have defined strong leadership. Qualities associated with women, such as compassion and compromise, have been linked with weak leadership. As the culture changes, and as more women enter the political elite, the popular notion of what it means to be a leader may also change, as people become accustomed to accepting more than one image of what a leader is or should be.

Many of the barriers to women's participation in the political elite are crumbling. The legal profession has traditionally been viewed as useful preparation for public office. As more women graduate from law school, more will be perceived as having the traditional qualifications for serving in the political elite. As more women run for and attain public office, women will increasingly be perceived as viable candidates and therefore attractive to potential donors. Political parties are also becoming more receptive to women candidates, and groups such as Emily's List are helping women overcome financial barriers to running for office. (Money has been referred to ironically as the "mother's milk" of American politics.)

Women now hold elective or appointive positions at all levels and in all three branches of government. A society in which, little more than a century ago, more than half of the population was disenfranchised now has universal suffrage, and blacks and women are becoming part of the political elite. A revolution has taken place, but the question now is, how far have women yet to go?

THE OUTLOOK FOR WOMEN: POSITIVE SIGNS, NEGATIVE PORTENTS

To better understand the fundamental changes that have occurred and to assess the progress that has been made, we should seek to determine the areas where women are making a difference and ascertain how they are doing so. Are they continuing to influence the outcome of elections, become a larger proportion of the political elite, and have an impact on public policy? What are the possible negative portents, such as opposition to some of the cultural changes that are taking place?

The 1994 Congressional Elections and Their Aftermath

In 1992 American voters elected record numbers of women to public office, as well as a president who was generally considered to be supportive of women's issues and who owed his electoral success in large measure to women voters. The congressional elections of 1994, however, presented a contradictory and possibly ominous message for women. Women's issues (such as child care and health care) were on the front burner from 1993 to mid-1994; Congress passed the Family and Medical Leave Act and four women were appointed to cabinet positions. Yet radio talk show hosts were denigrating women whose agendas differed from those of the political right and attacking First Lady Hillary Rodham Clinton. They concentrated on the problems that white males were having in the job market and in society in general, which were largely attributed to the increased opportunities that had been made available to women and minorities. Decrying quotas and reverse discrimination, they argued that it was unfair to penalize white males for the sins of past generations. Had the first lady's activism helped to mobilize "the revenge of the white male" in the 1994 congressional elections? Or were the attacks on her a reflection of the lack of support for Clinton administration policies? Mary Newsome, an editorial writer for the *Charlotte (N.C.) Observer,* explained: "Here's what gets people most about Hillary Clinton: She's openly smart, openly powerful and she's a feminist. She is richer and more powerful than virtually all American men, and this drives many of them, and many women nuts." Newsome pointed out that when you add those who do not like her politics and those opposed to her personality to those who object to the expansion of women's rights, "you've got a crowd," and added, "I don't think there's anything she can do to change this perception that she is a 'rhymes-with-rich' other than get some surgeon to carve out a chunk of her brain. And even that might not work, because too many people would still suspect her feminism." She suggested that women still meet a "cultural wall" in politics similar to the "glass ceiling" they sometimes encounter in the business world: "Maybe in 20 years Americans will be more willing to accept a first lady who is smart and powerful and who advises the president as openly as all those other non-elected advisers who happen to be male. (Who elected Ed Meese or H. R. Haldeman?) Maybe in 20 years. Maybe."[1]

In July 1994, Joan Steinau Lester described the contradictory images that plague women who actively participate in politics:

> Having a strong woman like Hillary Rodham Clinton in high visibility is a fascinating exercise in observing a string of contradictory stereotypes about women superimposed upon one person's features. . . . We never, any of us, have been able to imagine a strong woman orchestrating national policy [that is, both stimulating public debate on health care policy and participating in policy development]. . . . Our cultural landscape is changing so fast, however, it is hard to keep up. . . . One day she was a cold, steel-minded usurper of the presidency. The next day she was an airhead, searching naively for ways to do good. On the third day, when she presented that national health care plan to Congress, she ascended. With her "perfect" charm, sincerity and intellect, she was perceived as a modern day Eleanor Roosevelt. Flawless. A smart woman with all the edges sharpened. . . . And now, six months later: Whitewater, a crumbling health care plan and [Bob] Woodward's descriptions of Hillary's awesome power in the White House [*The Agenda: Inside the Clinton White House*]. An old female image is being called forth, one always at the ready: the Iron

Maiden. She is returning in the public mind to the earlier image as harsh usurper, a woman who bends all to her (unnatural) will.[2]

Republican candidates, capitalizing on the anti-government and anti-incumbency feelings generated by four decades of dominance by the Democratic Party, recaptured both houses of Congress, as well as a large number of governorships, and seats in state legislatures, and numerous positions in county and local government. The end result was the ability of Republicans to dominate the political debate and control the political agenda. Acting contrary to the accepted political wisdom that all politics is local in off-year congressional elections, the Republicans, led by then House minority whip Newt Gingrich, emphasized their theme of fundamental change in the operation of the federal government by formulating what they called a Contract with America. Whether the contract influenced the outcome of the elections is open to question, but congressional Republicans showed a willingness to follow through on many points of the contract that could have negative implications for women. The contract attempted to curtail many programs that had traditionally been important to women. It also sought to transfer to the states much of the power of the federal government (the level at which the rights of women and minorities have been expanded and their problems most frequently addressed). Despite their traditional dislike of "big government," Americans have long looked to the federal government to solve "big problems" that were national in scope or that state and local governments either could not or would not solve, such as providing a minimally secure retirement income for the elderly (Social Security), financial assistance to the poor (Medicare), and protection for the environment (the Clean Air Act). Some of the legislation passed by the previous Congress was reexamined, including the ban on assault weapons. The battle between the Democratic president and the Republican-controlled Congress over budget allocations ultimately led to the temporary closing down of the federal government.

By mid-1995, Democrats had begun to sense that public support for Republican proposals was waning. It began to appear that issues of relevance to women, children, the poor, and the elderly might be the focal point of the 1996 elections. Many believed that these elections would be a harbinger for women in politics. Would they spell defeat for the incumbent president, who had been so supportive of women's issues and appointed many women to positions of responsibility in his administration? Would

Hillary Clinton be a campaign issue? In their attempt to recapture Congress, would the Democrats be able to capitalize on public resentment as a result of the government shutdown and public fears about the possible cuts in entitlement programs? By November, ten women members of Congress either had decided to retire or had lost in the primaries. Would the number of women in Congress continue to decline?

Women's Key Role in the 1996 Elections

Since the beginning of the modern women's movement in the 1960s, women's political participation has increased significantly. The increase in voter turnout among women has created the potential for them to have a substantial impact on electoral outcomes. Women have had a higher voter turnout rate than men in all presidential election years after 1980. In 1964, nearly 5 percent more men voted than women. In 1992, 2.1 percent more women than men voted, and in 1996 the figure was 4.0 percent. Since 1986, women have also had a slightly higher voter turnout rate than men in mid-term elections.[3] Since the early 1980s, a gender gap has existed in vote choice for candidates. If there is a significant gender gap in both turnout and vote choice, women may determine the outcome of an election.[4] In every presidential election since 1980, women have been more likely than men to support the Democratic candidate.[5]

Women played an important role in the elections of 1996, especially the presidential election. After the election, Irene Natividad, of Women's Vote Project '96, commented that "women won this election even before the balloting began." Both presidential candidates actively courted women voters. During the campaign the candidates "tripped over themselves trying not to be mean" and were "trying to showcase the women in their parties, trying to influence the content of the conventions and debates." According to Natividad, women "have changed the political discourse."[6] Debbie Walsh, acting director of the Center for the American Woman and Politics, agreed: "Women made history in this election. They demonstrated the power of the gender gap and continued to make gains in high-level offices. The gender gap was the largest in history, topping the previous high of nine percent between Reagan and Mondale in 1984."[7]

Many have referred to it as a "gender chasm." President Clinton received 54 percent of the women's vote compared with Dole's 38 percent and independent candidate Ross Perot's 7 percent. As for men's votes, the difference between the two major candidates was minimal. Clinton received 43 per-

TABLE 7-1

Results of 1996 Presidential Election, by Gender and Age Group (percent)

Gender/Age	Clinton	Dole	Perot
Women			
18–29 years	58	31	9
30–44 years	54	37	7
45–59 years	52	40	7
60 years and older	53	41	5
Men			
18–29 years	47	38	12
30–44 years	41	46	10
45–59 years	44	43	10
60 years and older	43	48	8

Source: Exit polls reported in "Portrait of the Electorate," *New York Times,* November 10, 1996, 16.

cent, Dole received 44 percent, Perot received 10 percent. The gap in women's and men's votes for President Clinton was evident among all age groups, as shown in Table 7-1. Among independent voters, a group that can sometimes determine the outcome of a presidential election, men supported Clinton over Dole by 38 percent to 37 percent (a gap of 1 percent) whereas women preferred Clinton to Dole by 49 percent to 34 percent (a 15 percent gap). A gender gap in voting for Clinton rather than Dole also occurred in several marital, racial, and educational groups. Suburban men supported Dole (47 percent) over Clinton (41 percent); suburban women supported Clinton (53 percent) over Dole (39 percent). This significant gap was not surprising, since the issues that dominated the 1996 presidential election were, as in 1994, issues of concern to women. Working women may have been the key to the presidential election. Ellen R. Malcolm, president of Emily's List, observed that 1996 could be the year of the "angry woman voter": The "female counterpart of the 'angry white male'—the guy whose talk-radio-fueled anger dominated the 1994 election—is beginning to cause a commotion of her own. Alienated by the Republican 'revolution' on Capitol Hill and its attendant efforts to shred health, environmental, and social safety standards, she is hostile to the Republican Party [because of the stridency of the political discourse in Washington], but by no means a sure bet for Democrats." Citing a study by the Kaiser Family Foundation and Harvard University, Malcolm argued that women were less concerned with their own plight than with the prospects of others:

That sense of public mutuality and shared concern, that vision of America as a cooperative, rather than combative, community wasn't much in evidence in 1994. Instead, public displays of bravado over gun rights and punishing illegal immigrants dominated the campaign. But with literally millions of anxious and, yes, angry women's votes hanging in the balance, candidates who fail to address the concerns of women—concerns that extend beyond themselves to the precarious state of their families and their communities—can expect to come up short on votes in November. It is worth remembering that even though hotheaded Ralph always made the most noise on "The Honeymooners," it was Alice's slow-burning temper that packed the truly decisive punch.[8]

Women candidates won some highly visible congressional races in 1996. Although only 14 percent of all candidates for House seats were women, nearly one-third (7 of 22) of the challengers who defeated incumbents were women.[9] Women's increased participation was evident in the funding of political campaigns. The number of political action committees created to support women candidates increased from 4 in 1975–1976 to 48 in 1993 and 55 in 1996.[10] The provision of financial resources by women's PACs to women candidates early in the campaign cycle, thus enabling them to organize a professional staff, is no doubt one reason for the increased numbers of women winning elective office. After the 1996 elections, Malcolm announced: "We are thrilled that not one of our incumbent Democratic congresswomen lost. Our 45,000 Emily's List members proved why Democratic women have become such a potent force in American politics by contributing $6.5 million to elect women candidates and $3 million to mobilize voters as part of our Women Vote! project."[11]

The number of successful women candidates has increased in electoral contests at all levels—local, state, and federal. The proportion of members of Congress who are women increased from 4 percent in 1975 to nearly 12 percent at the beginning of the 105th Congress in 1997. Between 1974 and 1996, the proportion of women in statewide elective offices increased from 10 percent to 26 percent; the proportion of women in state legislative offices during the same period increased from 8 percent to 21 percent. However, the proportion of state legislators who are women varies from state to state. In 1996, the proportions were 3.6 percent in Alabama; 30.0 percent in Arizona, Oregon, and Vermont; 33.0 percent in Colorado; 34.9 percent in Nevada; and 39.5 percent in Washington (see Table 6-2). Women constituted at least 20 percent of the membership of state legislatures in 27 states in 1996.[12]

Although not directly related to the electoral success of women candidates, California's Proposition 209 is of interest to women. This proposition, which the voters approved by an 8 percent margin (54–46) on November 5, 1996, amends the California state constitution to prohibit the state from granting preferential treatment to any individual or group on the basis of race, sex, ethnicity, color, or national origin in the areas of public employment, education, or contracting. The ban also applies to all cities, counties, and public educational institutions. Although California is often considered a trend setter, supporters of affirmative action programs have downplayed the significance of the California vote. Mary Frances Berry, chair of the United States Commission on Civil Rights, pointed out that "this issue did not go anywhere in the Presidential campaign. It didn't seem to help Bob Dole. So for national politicians, there do not seem to be great benefits in pursuing the issue." Wade Henderson, executive director of the Leadership Conference on Civil Rights, argued that because women had emerged as a powerful force in the 1996 election, politicians might be wary of attacking affirmative action programs, which often benefit women.[13] Proposition 209 was subsequently challenged in the California courts but was upheld by the U.S. Court of Appeals for the Ninth Circuit on April 8, 1997. It could limit the opportunities made available to women in California under affirmative action programs. If this is indeed the result of similar actions in other states, then women may have to utilize the ballot box, as they did in the 1996 presidential race, to attempt to reverse such initiatives.

Political Elites and Policy Making

The increased number of women in the political elite has probably led to an increased awareness among men in public office that women's issues demand their attention. Women in elective office have influenced both the policy agenda and policy outcomes. With regard to policy agenda, women legislators are more likely to emphasize issues that are important to women, such as health care, care of the elderly, housing, and education, and to support state and federal equal rights amendments. They tend to be pro-choice on the abortion issue and to support the death penalty.[14] Both men and women in the legislatures recognize that women's efforts concerning these issues make a difference in legislative outcomes.[15] Women legislators may spend more time on, and allocate more staff to, constituency service activities.[16]

Men are more likely to name taxation and the budget as their most important legislative policy concerns. The degree to which women name women's issues as their top legislative priorities is related to ideology, occupation, age, and legislative seniority. (Such emphasis is more likely among liberals, women in traditionally female occupations, older women, and women who have served longer in the legislature.)[17] Women legislators from liberal districts are more supportive of women's issues than are men from liberal districts. However, women legislators from conservative districts are more supportive of such issues as health care and care for the elderly than are men from conservative districts. Democrats are more supportive of these issues than Republicans, but women legislators are more supportive than their male colleagues of the same party. African American women are more supportive of women's issues than are white women.[18]

Studies of state legislatures have found that women are more successful when they constitute more than a minimal percentage of a legislature's members—generally, at least 15 percent to 20 percent. The existence of a formal women's caucus in the legislature can also contribute to women's legislative success. Women can be more effective when they are appointed to leadership positions such as the head of a committee.[19] Women's legislative success is also a function of the number of campaign endorsements received from major women's groups and the number of legislators who are members of such groups.

With regard to policy outcomes, women members of Congress have obtained enactment of several policies that are particularly relevant to women. Beginning in 1990, the Congressional Caucus for Women's Issues sought enactment of major policy changes in health care research, provision of health care services, and disease prevention programs because of the significant gender-based inequities that existed in such programs and in the funding allocated to various types of medical research by the House and Senate Appropriations Committees. The Women's Health Equity Act, introduced in that year, included thirty-two specific health care initiatives. One proposal would require the inclusion of women subjects in research on illnesses afflicting both men and women. (Much of the prior research, such as clinical studies of heart disease, had included only men as subjects.) Another proposal would increase funding for research on health problems, such as breast cancer, that generally affect only women. Women serving on both the House and Senate Appropriations Committees and the relevant authorizing committees, such as the Senate Labor and Human Resources Committee, drafted this legislation, attempted to build support among male members of Congress for coalitions prior to committee and floor votes, and monitored the progress of legislation throughout the congressional process. Their efforts resulted in the establishment of major new research programs on lupus and breast cancer as well as the creation of the Office of Research on Women's Health in the National Institutes of Health in 1993.[20]

As might be expected, women and men voted differently on numerous issues in the 103d Congress (1993–1994). Although few in number (10 percent of both houses of Congress), women members significantly expanded the agenda and also influenced the content and discussion of legislation; thus they had a major impact on the policy outputs of that Congress.[21] The box on pages 144 and 145 presents some examples of legislation proposed by women representatives in the 104th Congress (1995–1996). The range of these policies demonstrates the influence that a critical mass of women can have on a legislature's priorities.

Sue Thomas has summarized three contributions of women in legislatures: raising issues previously considered to be of lesser significance, increasing societal acceptance of women in high-level positions, and presenting a wide range of ideas.

Female legislators have mastered legislative technique (as evidenced by their success in bill introduction and passage), proved their credibility by winning seats on the range of legislative committees and winning some leadership positions, demonstrated effectiveness in their role (as evidenced by their comparable reelection rate compared to men), increased their numbers, and succeeded in overcoming a great deal of the overt discrimination against them. . . . Although many benefits result from the direct efforts and successes of female legislators, arguably the most distinctive, dramatic, and fully developed contribution has been bringing issues that were heretofore considered marginal and of lesser significance squarely into the center of public agendas throughout the nation. These laws have transformed the lives and options of many people, and without women in elective office, it is doubtful that these benefits would be available today. . . . As women take their place as legitimate players on the political stage, society will likely become more tolerant of them in myriad positions of power: no longer will women in high-level, high-visibility positions be seen as exceptional. . . . It will allow young girls to grow up with the knowledge that women can perform all of society's roles and that their sex will not be a limitation on their dreams. . . . Increasing women's presence in the political sphere creates another benefit to public life generally:

EXAMPLES OF LEGISLATION PROPOSED BY WOMEN . . .

HEALTH

H.R. 173   *Medicaid Women's Basic Health Coverage Act of 1995*
Requires state Medicaid coverage of screening, mammographies, and pap smears for women age 35 and older.
Sponsored by Rep. Cardiss Collins (D–Ill.)

H.R. 641   *Women's Right to Know Act of 1995*
Prohibits government from limiting the receipt or provision of information about reproductive health care services.
Sponsored by Rep. Patricia Schroeder (D–Colo.)

H.R. 778   *Equal Access to Annual Screening Mammography Act of 1995*
Provides Medicare coverage for annual breast cancer screening for women age 65 and older.
Sponsored by Rep. Jane Harman (D–Calif.) and Rep. Barbara Vucanovich (R–Nev.)

H.R. 1721 *Ovarian Cancer Research and Information Amendments of 1995*
Authorizes funding for research on ovarian cancer. Specifies information to be included in ovarian cancer education programs.
Sponsored by Rep. Patsy Mink (D–Hawaii)

H.R. 1920 *Domestic Violence Victims Insurance Protection Act of 1995*
Prohibits insurers from denying or canceling insurance coverage solely because an individual has been a victim of domestic violence.
Sponsored by Rep. Susan Molinari (R–N.Y.)

H.R. 2435 *Self-Employed Health Fairness Act of 1995*
Increases the tax deduction for the health insurance costs of self-employed individuals to 100 percent.
Sponsored by Rep. Sue Kelly (R–N.Y.)

CHILDREN'S WELFARE

H.R. 195   *Interstate Child Support Enforcement Act*
Establishes a variety of measures to facilitate enforcement of child support.
Sponsored by Rep. Marge Roukema (R–N.J.)

H.R. 881   *Child Care Availability Incentives*
Allows tax credit for employers who provide qualified day care centers for their employees.
Sponsored by Rep. Deborah Pryce (R–Ohio)

CRIME

H.R. 174   *Gun Violence Economic Equity Act of 1995*
Holds the manufacturer, importer, or dealer of a handgun or an assault

. . . REPRESENTATIVES IN THE 104TH CONGRESS

weapon strictly liable for damages that result from the use of a handgun or an assault weapon, except when injury is suffered while committing a felony, is self-inflicted, or is a result of a discharge by a law enforcement officer or a member of the armed forces in the line of duty.

Sponsored by Rep. Cardiss Collins (D-Ill.)

EDUCATION

H.R. 1669 *Science and Mathematics Early Start Grant Program Act of 1995*

Provides funding for model programs that provide background instruction to Head Start personnel regarding the introduction of activities involving science and mathematics to children enrolled in Head Start programs.

Sponsored by Rep. Elizabeth Furse (D-Ore.)

GOVERNMENT REFORM

H.R. 2072 *Clean Congress Act of 1995*

Bans contributions to candidates in elections for federal office from anyone other than political party committees or individual residents of the candidate's home state. Bans gifts to members, officers, and employees of the House of Representatives. Limits personal loans by candidates to their campaigns to $5,000.

Sponsored by Rep. Linda Smith (R-Wash.)

H.R. 2545 *Voters Choice Act*

Allows states to adopt proportional representation rather than single-member "winner take all" districts. Proposes a system of representation similar to that used in many European nations.

Sponsored by Rep. Cynthia McKinney (D-Ga.)

ECONOMY

H.R. 1019 *Microenterprise Opportunity Expansion Act*

Encourages the proliferation of microenterprise by allowing Social Security and unemployment recipients to start small businesses, treating grants and loans to certain microenterprises as community reinvestments, and requiring federal banking agencies to establish a division to promote microenterprises.

Sponsored by Rep. Cardiss Collins (D-Ill.)

H.R. 1507 *Fair Pay Act of 1995*

Prohibits discrimination in payment of wages on the basis of sex, race, or national origin.

Sponsored by Rep. Eleanor Holmes Norton (D-D.C.)

access to a greater diversity of ideas and experiences that fuel definition of problems and the creation of solutions. Leaving any group out of policy formation and legitimization necessarily means that the range of ideas is artificially limited. It is hard to imagine a worse way to restrict the visions of a society.[22]

Women in public office exhibit a leadership style that encourages the inclusion of other perspectives. Women are also more likely to emphasize and attempt to increase citizen participation in the policy-making process, particularly that of formerly excluded or underrepresented groups such as women and minorities.[23] Furthermore, women elected officials tend to make special efforts to hire women and to recruit them as candidates for public office.[24] Women governors and mayors tend to appoint more women to their staffs and to boards and commissions that are important in the making, implementation, and enforcement of policy. A study of mayors (both men and women) in five large cities found that women tend to place greater emphasis on teamwork and collegiality.[25]

Until the 1980s, few women were attorneys, and very few were judges. The increased enrollment of women in law schools as a consequence of passage of the Higher Education Act Amendments of 1972 resulted in a gradual increase in the proportion of attorneys who are women and thus in the number of women appointed as judges at the municipal, state, and federal levels. President Jimmy Carter nominated 40 women for federal judgeships—more women than were appointed by any prior president. However, by the end of his term in early 1981, only 46 women were serving as federal judges. During President Ronald Reagan's eight years in office, he nominated only 26 women for federal judgeships, although there were 368 vacancies during that time. He did appoint the first woman—Sandra Day O'Connor—to the Supreme Court. President George Bush appointed fewer women to fill judicial vacancies than did President Reagan.[26] During President Bill Clinton's first year in office, more than 40 percent of his nominees for federal judicial appointments were women.[27] But by July 1995, only 16 percent of the federal judges were women.[28]

Women judges do make a difference in terms of the decisions they render. They are more likely than male judges to treat women lawyers trying cases in their courts in a nondiscriminatory manner and to decide in favor of women litigants in cases dealing with gender-related issues such as maternity leave, the rights of battered women, and sexual harassment at the place of employment.[29]

MAKING A DIFFERENCE:
TWO PATHS TO POLITICS

In late 1996, the names of two very different women were in the news—Carolyn McCarthy and Madeleine Albright. Their stories provide good examples of the different routes women have taken to politics and the impact that women can have on society.

Carolyn McCarthy's path to politics was marked by tragedy. A Long Island homemaker, she had taken "no part in local politics and barely kept abreast of the daily ideological tussle in Washington. She concentrated on family: her husband, Dennis McCarthy, and her son, Kevin. Both McCarthy men commuted by Long Island Rail Road to jobs in Manhattan." In December 1993, her husband was killed and her son seriously wounded on a commuter train by Colin Ferguson, who had boarded the train with a nine-millimeter semiautomatic handgun and a duffel bag filled with ammunition. Ferguson shot a total of twenty-five people, six of whom later died. After his trial, Carolyn McCarthy became an antigun activist. The *New York Times* noted that her "simple questions tested the complications surrounding the issue. Why do ordinary citizens need assault weapons? Why are guns so easy to obtain? She was earnest rather than slick, and her message carried resonance." At the beginning of 1996 Congressman Daniel Frisa, who represented her district, voted to repeal a ban on nineteen specific types of assault weapons. After questioning him about his vote and being dissatisfied with his response (that the legislation was flawed), McCarthy decided to run against him. Although she was a Republican, the Republican Party officials she contacted were not interested in a divisive primary. The Democrats, however, were eager to have a viable candidate in an overwhelmingly Republican congressional district. In the election campaign, Frisa described McCarthy as a "one-issue lightweight"; she countered that "her kind of common sense is woefully absent in Washington." On election night, wearing a button proclaiming that "When women vote, women win," McCarthy celebrated a sixteen percentage point victory (57–41) over Frisa. Tricia Primrose, a spokeswoman for the Democratic Congressional Campaign Committee, said that "when you see Carolyn McCarthy win so resoundingly, it reaffirms our belief in the political process. This was someone who was unhappy with what was happening in Washington, who took a stand and ran for Congress. She's going to shake the place up. She's going to tell it like it is." [30]

In January 1997, the Senate ratified Madeleine Albright's nomination as

FOR FURTHER EXPLORATION: WOMEN IN POLITICS
ON THE WORLD WIDE WEB

Many web sites have been created to supply information about women and politics and women's issues. Some are located at academic institutions such as the Center for the American Woman and Politics at Rutgers University. Sites have been created by political parties, government organizations, private enterprises, and individuals; they may provide "hot buttons" to many other sites. It should be remembered, however, that web sites can change rapidly.

www.cc.rochester.edu:80/SBA/95-75/	Susan B. Anthony Center University of Rochester Rochester, N.Y.
www.ffconnect.com	*Forefront: The Magazine for Influential Women*
www.rci.rutgers.edu/~cawp	Center for the American Woman and Politics Eagleton Institute of Politics Rutgers University New Brunswick, N.J.
www.feminist.org/gateway/po_exec2.html	Feminist Internet Gateway
www.emilyslist.org/home.htm	Emily's List
www. igc.apc.org/women/feminist.html	Feminist Activist Resources on the Net
www.feminist.com/nwpc.htm	National Women's Political Caucus
www. electriciti.com/~lwvus	League of Women Voters
www.yale.edu/wcsyale/	Women's Campaign School Yale University New Haven, Conn.

secretary of state in the second Clinton administration. The secretary of state is fourth in line of succession to the presidency, after the vice president, the Speaker of the House of Representatives, and the president pro tempore of the Senate. Albright came to the position with impressive credentials, including a distinguished career in academia. She had been an assistant to Sen. Edmund Muskie, director of the Women in Foreign Service Program at Georgetown University, a member of the U.S. delegation to the United Nation's Women's Conference in Beijing, and U.S. ambassador to the United Nations. President Clinton praised the woman who was born in Czechoslovakia and whose family had fled from the Nazis for her "steely determination"; he also denied that he was appointing her to satisfy women's groups. He said that of all the candidates for the position, "she had the best combination of qualities to succeed and to serve our country at this moment in history." [31] In December 1996, *Boston Globe* columnist Ellen Goodman had pointed out that "some folks huffed that her nomination as secretary of state was just 'politics'. Others said the president was just 'paying back' women's groups. Such is the fate of her generation of women. Once upon a time they were banned from the top jobs on account of gender. When they finally make it, somebody is sure to say that they got the job because of their gender." [32] Goodman's comment emphasizes what many women recognize—that even when women succeed on their own merits, some still question whether they were really the best candidates. Perhaps when the appointment of women to high office is viewed as a common occurrence, such questions will cease.

Goodman raised another question regarding the impact of Madeleine Albright:

> With all this skittishness about the "woman thing," not even her supporters have been eager to discuss the upside of this first. What might this woman, as a woman, bring to the foreign policy job? Not merely by her presence, but by her point of view, her peripheral vision? Albright herself has never been reticent to see her own life in the context of the woman's movement. In another time, as she likes to say, "the only way I might have found to influence foreign policy is by marrying a diplomat and then pouring tea on an offending ambassador's lap."

Albright can use her position to focus world attention on the injustices to women and push for women's rights; thus she can influence the status and treatment of women and children throughout the world. With the rise of Islamic fundamentalism, which requires that women play a subservient role in society, and the breakup of the former Soviet Union, which was followed by a number of civil wars, women's rights have been imperiled. Indeed, rape has often been used as a form of political intimidation. Goodman points out that

> in foreign policy, the idea that women's rights are human rights [is] new and radical. It's only since the disasters in Bosnia and Rwanda that rape was

defined as a crime of war, rather than a fact of war. . . . You won't need to explain to this secretary of state why rape is a war crime. In her friend Sen. Barbara Mikulski's phrase, "She not only understands what happens to women in war and in sweatshops and in brothels, but she can articulate it in foreign-policy terms." . . . In another first, the United Nations condemned the Taliban in Afghanistan [in October 1996] for issuing decrees that would put women back in their old place. In Albright's blunt words, the Taliban would "essentially deprive women of all rights, except the right to remain silent, indoors, uneducated and invisible."

An interesting question is whether a choice will ever have to be made between the universal interests of women, who constitute more that one-half of the world's population, and U.S. national interests—for example, maintaining the flow of oil in the Middle East, where the rights of women are being violated. Goodman argues that

> in this new world, one of the goals of foreign aid and policy is to empower stable, middle-class democracies. We have begun to recognize that you can't get there without education and birth control for women. . . . I am not suggesting that Albright will or should be a Secretary of the Female State. . . . But I am suggesting that her gender may broaden the current outlook. When Albright looks down the list of appointments, new names may come to the top. When she looks down the list of international woes—as far down as sexual slavery or child labor or genital mutilation— new priorities may arise. And when this woman represents the United States of America to other continents and cultures where women are still the poorest and most illiterate citizens, the world may look a little different.

Since passage of the Nineteenth Amendment, women's role in the political process has changed dramatically. Especially since the mid-1960s, women's opportunities in the areas of education and employment have increased, and women have taken advantage of them. Although women do not yet have equal representation in all of the policy-making institutions, they no longer have to knock on the doors to political power. At all levels and in all three branches of government, women are making a difference.

NOTES

1. Mary Newsome, "What Gets People about Hillary," *Dayton Daily News,* January 18, 1995, 11A. In January 1995, the mother of Newt Gingrich, the new

Speaker of the House, confided to CBS news anchor Connie Chung in a television interview that he had called Hillary Rodham Clinton a bitch.

2. Joan Steinau Lester, "Hillary Hit with Conflicting Stereotypes," *Dayton Daily News,* July 5, 1994, 7A.

3. Center for the American Woman and Politics, *Sex Differences in Voter Turnout* (New Brunswick, N.J.: Eagleton Institute of Politics, Rutgers University, August 1993), fact sheet.

4. In 1992, women's vote choices differed sufficiently from those of men to result in electoral victory for the women candidates (Democrats Dianne Feinstein and Barbara Boxer) in both of California's contests for the U.S. Senate. Sometimes, however, the gender gap is reversed, as in the 1992 senatorial race between Les AuCoin and Bob Packwood in Oregon; only 44 percent of the women but 60 percent of the men supported Packwood, who won the election. Center for the American Woman and Politics, *The Gender Gap,* August 1994, fact sheet. Senator Packwood's resignation, effective October 1, 1995, followed a thirty-three-month inquiry by the Senate Ethics Committee into his alleged abuse of office, obstruction of justice, and sexual misconduct. *Congressional Quarterly Weekly Report,* January 6, 1996, 21.

5. Center for the American Woman and Politics, *The Gender Gap,* July 1992, fact sheet. In 1992, men were significantly more likely than women to support third-party candidate Ross Perot. In the American National Election Study postelection survey, 16 percent of the white women and 26 percent of the white men reported voting for Perot. Only 3 percent of African Americans reported voting for Perot. See Paul R. Abramson, John H. Aldrich, and David W. Rohde, *Change and Continuity in the 1992 Elections,* rev. ed. (Washington, D.C.: CQ Press, 1995), Table 5-1, 133.

6. Quoted in Mimi Hall, "Women Roared, and Candidates Listened," *USA Today,* November 7, 1996, 2A. Accompanying Republican presidential candidate Bob Dole on the campaign trail was his wife, Elizabeth, who had an impressive record of public service, including secretary of transportation and director of the American Red Cross.

7. Center for the American Woman and Politics, "Women Make News as Voters, Edge Upward as Officeholders," November 7, 1996. This press release is available from the Internet: http://rci.rutgers.edu/~cawp/candprss.html.

8. Ellen R. Malcolm, "The 'Angry Woman Voter' May Change '96 Elections," *Philadelphia Inquirer,* March 8, 1996. Article is available from the Internet: http://www.emilyslist.org/talk/press3.htm.

9. "Women Make News as Voters."

10. Susan Roberts, "Women's PACs: Evolution, Operation, and Outlook." Paper prepared for presentation at the 1992 meeting of the Southern Political Science Association, Atlanta. See also Center for the American Woman and Politics, *News and Notes* 9 (2): 18, and 10 (3): 6.

11. "A Great Election Night for Emily's List and Democratic Women," November 6, 1996; press release available from the Internet: http://www.emilyslist.org/news/press/110696.htm.

12. Center for the American Woman and Politics, *Women in Elective Office 1996,* February 1996, fact sheet.

13. Robert Pear, "In California, Foes of Affirmative Action See a New Day," *New York Times,* November 7, 1996, B7.

14. Sue Thomas and Susan Welch, "The Impact of Gender on Activities and Priorities of State Legislators," *Western Political Quarterly* 44 (June 1991): 445–457; Sue Thomas, "The Impact of Women on State Legislative Policies," *Journal of Politics* 53 (November 1991): 958–966; Debra L. Dodson and Susan J. Carroll, *Reshaping the Agenda:Women in State Legislatures* (New Brunswick, N.J.: Center for the American Woman and Politics, Eagleton Institute of Politics, Rutgers University, 1991), 5.

15. Dodson and Carroll, *Reshaping the Agenda,* 12.

16. Sue Thomas, "The Effects of Race and Gender on Constituency Service," *Western Political Quarterly* 44 (March 1992): 169–180.

17. Dodson and Carroll, *Reshaping the Agenda,* chap. 3.

18. Thomas, "Impact of Women"; Dodson and Carroll, *Reshaping the Agenda,* chap. 2.

19. Jeanie R. Stanley and Diane D. Blair, "Gender Differences in Legislative Effectiveness: The Impact of the Legislative Environment," in Debra L. Dodson, ed., *Gender and Policymaking* (New Brunswick, N.J.: Center for the American Woman and Politics, Eagleton Institute of Politics, Rutgers University, 1991), 115–129.

20. Debra L. Dodson, Susan J. Carroll, Ruth B. Mandel, Katherine E. Kleeman, Ronnee Schreiber, and Debra Liebowitz, *Voices, Views, Votes: The Impact of Women in the 103rd Congress* (New Brunswick, N.J.: Center for the American Woman and Politics, Eagleton Institute of Politics, Rutgers University, 1995).

21. Ibid.

22. Sue Thomas, *How Women Legislate* (New York: Oxford University Press, 1994), 139–147.

23. Susan J. Carroll, Debra L. Dodson, and Ruth B. Mandel, *The Impact of Women in Public Office* (New Brunswick, N.J.: Center for the American Woman and Politics, Eagleton Institute of Politics, Rutgers University, 1991); Janet Boles, "Advancing the Women's Agenda within Local Legislatures: The Role of Female Elected Officials," in Dodson, *Gender and Policymaking,* 39–48.

24. Dodson and Carroll, *Reshaping the Agenda,* 3.

25. Sue Tolleson-Rinehart, "Do Women Leaders Make a Difference? Substance, Style, and Perceptions," in ibid., 93–102.

26. Nancy E. McGlen and Karen O'Connor, *Women, Politics, and American Society* (Englewood Cliffs, N.J.: Prentice-Hall, 1995), 91–92.

27. *American Bar Association Journal,* April 1994, 16.

28. H. T. Smith, "President's Page," *American Bar Association Journal,* July 1995, 8.

29. Elaine Martin, "Judicial Gender and Judicial Choices," in Dodson, *Gender and Policymaking,* 49–61.

30. Dan Barry, "L. I. Widow's Story: Next Stop, Washington," *New York Times,* November 7, 1996, B14.

31. "Clinton Names Albright Secretary of State," from Reuters NewMedia, PointCast Network, December 6, 1996.

32. Ellen Goodman, "Albright Selection More Than a 'First'," *Dayton Daily News,* December 14, 1996, 11A. (Goodman's column originally appeared in the *Boston Globe.*)

Index